cooking
japanese

cooking
japanese

whitecap

contents

a visual and culinary feast

The popularity of Japanese cuisine continues to grow around the world, thanks to its fresh palate-pleasing tastes and health-giving attributes. While Japanese restaurant dishes can be truly tantalizing, attempting to re-create them at home can seem a little intimidating. However, the preparation techniques are really quite simple, so once familiar with a few major ingredients, along with some of the cooking methods and styles of presentation, it is possible to make this exotic cuisine seem a little less daunting.

Around the centrepiece of rice, a huge variety of dishes are created utilizing the freshest of ingredients, with vegetables and seafood playing far more frequent roles than meat. The natural and true flavours of the individual foods are never overwhelmed, but rather enhanced, by any added ingredients.

Although Japan is no longer a predominantly agrarian nation, the rhythm of the seasons still resounds through Japanese life. Many people continue to nurture a deep appreciation of nature, and that is partly reflected in their eager anticipation and enjoyment of seasonal foods. A great variety of the wild 'fruits' of both the land and sea complement Japan's cultivated food products. The brief period when any particular food is at the peak of its flavour is referred to as *shun*, and the Japanese await with great anticipation the arrival of their favourites through the year. It may be the bamboo shoots of spring, the sweetfish of summer called *ayu*, autumn's celebrated *matsutake* mushrooms, winter's *mikan* or tangerines, or any of dozens of other seasonal delights.

The culinary 'principles of five' guide the Japanese cook in creating a healthful, varied and appealing meal. The rule of five colours assures not only visual appeal but serves to increase nutritional variety. The use of five tastes offers a contrast of sweet, sour, salty, bitter and spicy. Aside from leaving ingredients raw, the five ways of preparation are comprised of pickling, simmering, steaming, grilling (broiling) and frying. Each of the five senses is also to be considered. And the principle of five outlooks adds a spiritual component to the pleasure of dining, based on traditional Buddhist precepts about food.

Japanese cuisine is truly unique in all the world. It is a cuisine of subtle yet sometimes surprising and even magical flavours. *Cooking Japanese* helps you bring those wonderful flavours home to your very own table.

soups and starters

One can hardly overstate the significance of soup in Japan, for in the time-honoured Japanese meal pattern, miso soup (or occasionally a clear soup) has long been an essential — at breakfast, lunch and dinner — accompanying a variety of other dishes. This delicious and nutritious soup is enriched with one or two added ingredients such as seaweed, mushrooms, seasonal vegetables, tofu or tiny shellfish. The typical covered lacquer bowl in which it is served keeps the soup hot and preserves its fine aroma. To consume such soup properly, the solid ingredients are picked out and eaten with chopsticks, while the soup is sipped directly from the bowl.

Noodle dishes are also often prepared in a soup base, and are very popular as a quick but filling one-bowl workday lunch or a snack after a late night out. Buckwheat noodles called *soba*, thick and chewy wheat noodles called *udon*, and Chinese-style wheat noodles called *ramen* are commonly served in a broth flavoured with soy sauce, although regional and personal preferences sometimes call for other broths. There are any number of toppings, from the simplest of spring onion (scallion) slivers to chunks of tofu, deep-fried tempura, greens and a variety of other vegetables, slices of pork or even a raw egg yolk.

The foundation of most Japanese soups is *dashi*, a flavourful sea broth made from *konbu* (kelp) alone in its vegetarian version, but most often with added shavings of smoky dried bonito (*katsuobushi*). So easy and quick it is to make from scratch, that one need not resort to the use of instant *dashi* granules unless extremely pressed for time or lacking the basic ingredients.

Although in a traditional Japanese meal nearly everything is placed in front of the diners at the same time, there are many individual dishes that make ideal starters when Western style courses are being served. Indeed, Japanese cuisine offers numerous kinds of tasty titbits that readily lend themselves to such an appetizer role. Among them is tofu, which shows its versatility in the many different ways it can be prepared — fresh and chilled, hot in broth, deep-fried, pan-fried or grilled (broiled) — and further by its sauces and garnishes. Meat-filled dumplings, spring rolls or seafood-and-vegetable fritters serve as wonderful savoury bites to start off a meal, as do bite-sized morsels of meat, poultry and seafood, seasoned and prepared in traditional Japanese ways.

udon noodles in broth . . . . serves 4

NOODLES IN DASHI ARE AS MUCH A COMFORT FOOD FOR JAPANESE AS CHICKEN NOODLE SOUP IS FOR MANY WESTERNERS. WHILE SIMPLICITY ITSELF, THIS DISH OFFERS COMPLEX FLAVOURS AND TEXTURES — SWEET AND SALTY, SMOKY AND SPICY, AND SLIGHTLY CHEWY WITH A BIT OF CRUNCH.

dashi II	1.5 litres (52 fl oz/6 cups) (see recipe on page 24)
spring onions (scallions)	3, 2 cut into 4 cm (1 1/2 in) lengths, 1 thinly sliced on the diagonal
mirin	60 ml (2 fl oz/1/4 cup)
shoyu (Japanese soy sauce)	60 ml (2 fl oz/1/4 cup)
sugar	2 teaspoons
fresh udon noodles	400 g (14 oz)
shichimi togarashi (seven-spice mix)	to serve, optional

Pour the dashi into a large saucepan and bring to the boil over medium–high heat. Reduce to a simmer.

Add the lengths of spring onion to the dashi along with the mirin, shoyu and sugar and stir to combine. Simmer over low heat for 5 minutes.

Meanwhile, bring a large saucepan of lightly salted water to the boil, add the noodles and cook, stirring gently, for 5 minutes, or until tender. Drain well and rinse. Divide the noodles among four warmed serving bowls. Top with the thinly sliced spring onion. Ladle the broth over the top. If you like, pass around the shichimi togarashi for sprinkling.

Udon are soft, thick wheat noodles, made from flour, water and salt. Although well loved all over the country, udon are particularly popular in the area around Osaka. Today most udon noodles are commercially made — when home-made, the dough requires quite forceful kneading, often best accomplished by foot stomping. Udon are sometimes served cold with a dipping sauce in summer, but are most often eaten in a hot broth. Toppings can be simply a raw egg, slivers of *abura-age* (deep-fried tofu), wakame seaweed or tempura. The noodles are available fresh, semi-dried and dried.

agedashi tofu......................................

FOR THIS RECIPE THE TOFU IS COATED WITH POTATO STARCH, THEN BRIEFLY DEEP-FRIED. THE OPTIONAL ADDITION OF SESAME OIL TO THE FRYING OIL WILL ENRICH THE FLAVOUR, WHILE THE FRESH, COOL GARNISHES PROVIDE PLEASANT CONTRAST TO THE WARM TOFU AND BROTH.

silken firm tofu	600 g (1 lb 5 oz) block
vegetable oil	for deep-frying
sesame oil	60 ml (2 fl oz/¼ cup), optional
potato starch	for coating
daikon	70 g (2½ oz), peeled, finely grated, then squeezed to remove excess liquid
fresh ginger	2 teaspoons finely grated
spring onion (scallion)	thinly sliced, to garnish
nori flakes	to garnish

sauce

dashi II	170 ml (5½ fl oz/⅔ cup) (see recipe on page 24)
shoyu (Japanese soy sauce)	2 tablespoons
sake	1 tablespoon
mirin	1 tablespoon

Be very careful when working with the tofu — it is very soft and breaks easily. To weight the tofu, first wrap it in a clean tea towel (dish towel). Put two plates on top of the tofu and leave for about 30 minutes to extract any excess moisture. Remove the tofu from the tea towel, cut into eight pieces, then pat dry with paper towels.

To make the sauce, combine all the ingredients in a small saucepan. Bring to the boil over high heat, then reduce the heat to very low to keep the sauce warm until ready to use.

Fill a deep-fat fryer or large saucepan one-third full of vegetable oil, then add the sesame oil, if using. Heat to 180°C (350°F), or until a cube of bread dropped into the oil browns in 15 seconds.

Lightly coat the tofu with the potato starch and then deep-fry in batches for about 3 minutes, or until the tofu just starts to become a pale golden colour around the edges. Drain well on paper towels, then divide the tofu among four individual bowls (or one large, wide bowl). Carefully pour the sauce into the bowl. Top the tofu with a little daikon and ginger and garnish with the spring onion and nori flakes. Eat with chopsticks and, if you need one, a spoon.

Wrap the tofu in a tea towel and put two plates on top

Lightly coat the tofu pieces with the potato starch

Deep-fry the tofu until it starts to turn pale golden

deep-fried prawns with dipping sauce

.... serves 4

FAMILIAR BREADED PRAWNS (SHRIMP) ARE ELEVATED HERE THROUGH THE USE OF PANKO, WHICH IS USED FOR ITS DELICATE FLAKINESS, AND YIELDS A LIGHT AND CRISPY CRUST. PICKLED JAPANESE CUCUMBERS AND MITSUBA GIVE THE DIPPING SAUCE A PARTICULARLY EASTERN FLAVOUR AND PIQUANCY.

raw large prawns (shrimp)	20, peeled, deveined, tails intact
plain (all-purpose) flour	30 g (1 oz/¼ cup), for coating
ground white pepper	¼ teaspoon
egg	1
panko (Japanese breadcrumbs)	60 g (2¼ oz/1 cup)
vegetable oil	for deep-frying
sesame oil	60 ml (2 fl oz/¼ cup)
lemon wedges	to serve

dipping sauce

Japanese mayonnaise	170 g (6 oz/⅔ cup)
pickled Japanese cucumber or dill pickles	1½ tablespoons finely chopped
Japanese rice vinegar	1 tablespoon
spring onion (scallion)	1, white part only, finely chopped
mitsuba or flat-leaf (Italian) parsley	2 tablespoons chopped
garlic	1 clove, crushed
ground white pepper	pinch

Make three cuts in the belly of each prawn. Turn the prawn over and, starting from the tail end, press down gently at intervals along its length — this helps to break the connective tissue, preventing the prawns from curling up too much.

Season the flour with ¼ teaspoon salt and the white pepper. Break the egg into a bowl, add 2 teaspoons water and lightly beat together. Holding the prawns by their tails so the tails remain uncoated, lightly coat them with the seasoned flour, then dip into the egg, allowing any excess to drip off. Finally, coat with the panko, pressing on the crumbs to help them adhere. Refrigerate the prawns until you are ready to cook.

To make the dipping sauce, put all the ingredients in a small bowl and stir to combine. Season to taste with salt and white pepper. Refrigerate until ready to serve.

Fill a deep-fat fryer or large saucepan one-third full of vegetable oil and add the sesame oil. Heat to 180°C (350°F), or until a cube of bread dropped into the oil browns in 15 seconds. Deep-fry the prawns in batches for 2 minutes, or until golden. Drain on paper towels and serve immediately accompanied with the dipping sauce and lemon wedges.

Press down along the length of the prawn to flatten it a little

Coat the prawn with the flour, then dip it into the egg

Coat the prawn with the panko, pressing to adhere the crumbs

noodle-coated prawns .... serves 4

TENDER SWEET PRAWNS (SHRIMP) ARE GIVEN A SURPRISING CRUNCH WHEN BUNDLED INTO A JACKET OF SOMEN NOODLES AND SECURED WITH AN *OBI*, OR SASH, OF NORI. THIS ATTRACTIVE PRESENTATION MAKES THESE NOT ONLY AN APPEALING AND DELICIOUS STARTER, BUT IDEAL FINGER FOOD FOR A PARTY.

raw large prawns (shrimp)	12, peeled, deveined, tails intact
dried somen noodles	200 g (7 oz)
nori sheet	1/2, cut into strips 7 cm (2 3/4 in) long and 1.5 cm (5/8 in) wide
vegetable oil	for deep-frying

batter

plain (all-purpose) flour	250 g (9 oz/2 cups)
egg yolks	2
iced water	500 ml (17 fl oz/2 cups)

soy and ginger sauce

fresh ginger	1 tablespoon grated
sugar	2 teaspoons
shoyu (Japanese soy sauce)	250 ml (9 fl oz/1 cup)

Make three cuts in the belly of each prawn. Turn the prawn over and, starting from the tail end, press down gently at intervals along its length — this helps to break the connective tissue, preventing the prawns from curling up too much.

To make the batter, put the flour, egg yolks and water in a bowl and whisk until just combined. Break the noodles so they are the same length as the prawns, not including the tails, and put them on a board. Dip each prawn into the batter, lay it on the noodles and gather up to cover the prawns, pressing the noodles so they stick to the prawn. Wrap a nori strip around the centre of each prawn, dampen the ends with a little water and press to seal.

Fill a deep-fat fryer or large saucepan one-third full of vegetable oil. Heat to 180°C (350°F), or until a cube of bread dropped into the oil browns in 15 seconds. Deep-fry the prawns in batches for 2–3 minutes, or until golden. To make the soy and ginger sauce, combine the ingredients in a bowl and mix well. Serve the prawns with the sauce, for dipping.

While other Japanese noodles are sold both fresh and dried, somen are only available dried. During their manufacture these white wheat noodles are lightly oiled and stretched into the finest strands before being air-dried and packaged. They are cooked only briefly and usually served cold. In the heat of summer, they are often served in a bowl of iced water, garnished with a few slices of cucumber and tomato, and perhaps a prawn (shrimp), with a light dipping sauce on the side. *Nagashi somen* is an entertaining speciality in which small clumps of noodles flow down a flume from kitchen to table, to be snatched up by diners with their chopsticks.

gyoza..makes 30

THESE TASTY MORSELS MAKE A GREAT STARTER, EXCEPT FOR THE FACT THAT THOSE FEW BITES MAY LEAVE YOUR GUESTS LONGING FOR MORE. A LITTLE PRACTICE SOON YIELDS DEFTLY PLEATED EDGES, ALTHOUGH A LITTLE JAPANESE CRIMPING TOOL EXISTS PRECISELY TO SIMPLIFY THIS TASK.

filling

Chinese cabbage	200 g (7 oz), stems removed, finely chopped
minced (ground) pork	200 g (7 oz)
fresh ginger	2 teaspoons finely grated
garlic	3 cloves, crushed
shoyu (Japanese soy sauce)	1 1/2 tablespoons
sake	2 teaspoons
mirin	2 teaspoons
ground white pepper	1/4 teaspoon
spring onions (scallions)	2, finely chopped

dipping sauce

Japanese rice vinegar	80 ml (2 1/2 fl oz/1/3 cup)
shoyu (Japanese soy sauce)	80 ml (2 1/2 fl oz/1/3 cup)
sesame oil or chilli sesame oil	2 teaspoons
gyoza wrappers	200 g (7 oz) packet
vegetable oil	for pan-frying, plus an extra 2 teaspoons
sesame oil	2 teaspoons
Japanese mustard	to serve, optional

To make the filling, put the cabbage in a colander, sprinkle with salt and set aside for 30 minutes. Squeeze well, transfer to a bowl and mix with the rest of the filling ingredients.

Meanwhile, to make the dipping sauce, put all the ingredients in a small bowl and stir to combine. Divide among small dishes.

Lay a wrapper in the palm of your hand and put 2 teaspoons of filling in the middle. Lightly dampen the edge of the wrapper with water, then fold the edges together to form a semicircle, pressing firmly to enclose the filling. Dampen the curved edge of the wrapper, then fold along the edge to make overlapping pleats. Put each gyoza on a tray lined with plastic wrap. Repeat with the remaining wrappers and filling. Refrigerate until ready to cook.

Heat a little oil in a large, non-stick frying pan over medium–high heat. Put the gyoza in the pan, flat side down, in a single layer, leaving a little space between each (cook in batches if your pan is not large enough). Cook for 2 minutes, or until the bottoms are crisp and golden. Combine 125 ml (4 fl oz/1/2 cup) boiling water with the extra vegetable oil and sesame oil, then add to the pan. Cover, reduce the heat to low and cook for 10 minutes. Remove the lid, increase the heat to high and continue to cook until the liquid has evaporated, making sure the gyoza don't catch and burn. Remove from the pan and drain on paper towels. Serve with the dipping sauce.

Put 2 teaspoons of the filling in the middle of the wrapper

Dampen the curved edge, then fold in half to form a semicircle

Fold pleats around the curved edge to form a dumpling

tofu steaks with mushrooms
....serves 8

PREPARED IN BUTTER AND TOPPED WITH TWO KINDS OF MUSHROOMS, TOFU TAKES ON A RICHER, SAVOURY FLAVOUR. THESE VEGETARIAN 'STEAKS', IDEAL AS STARTERS IN SMALL PORTIONS, COULD ALSO BE SERVED AS A MAIN DISH ACCOMPANIED WITH A LIGHT SALAD.

firm (cotton) tofu	600 g (1 lb 5 oz) block
butter	25 g (1 oz)
sesame oil	1 teaspoon
garlic	2 cloves, crushed
fresh ginger	2 teaspoons finely grated
spring onions (scallions)	5, 4 sliced on the diagonal into 4 cm (1½ in) lengths, 1 thinly sliced on the diagonal
fresh shimeji mushrooms	150 g (5½ oz), pulled apart in small clumps
fresh shiitake mushrooms	150 g (5½ oz), stems discarded, caps thickly sliced
vegetable oil	1 tablespoon
ground white pepper	pinch
sansho pepper	pinch
shoyu (Japanese soy sauce)	2 tablespoons
mirin	2 tablespoons

To weight the tofu, first wrap it in a clean tea towel (dish towel). Put two plates on top of the tofu and leave for about 1 hour to extract any excess moisture. Remove from the tea towel, then pat dry with paper towels. Cut the block in half horizontally so you have two thin slices. Cut each of these slices into quarters so you have eight even cubes in total. Set aside.

Heat half the butter and half the sesame oil in a large, heavy-based frying pan over medium–high heat. Add the garlic, ginger, lengths of spring onion, shimeji and shiitake mushrooms to the pan. Cook for 3–4 minutes, or until the mushrooms are softened. Remove from the pan.

Add the remaining butter and sesame oil with the vegetable oil to the pan. Season the tofu steaks with salt, white pepper and sansho pepper and cook for about 6 minutes on each side, or until golden. Remove from the pan, cover and set aside.

Pour out the excess oil from the pan, leaving about 1 teaspoon. Increase the heat to high and add the shoyu and mirin, then return the mushroom mixture to the pan. Mix well and cook for 2 minutes, or until the mushrooms are heated through. Top each piece of tofu with the mushroom mixture and garnish with the sliced spring onion. Serve immediately. Serve with rice and green vegetables or a salad.

Pull the shimeji mushrooms apart in small clumps

Cook the garlic, ginger, spring onions and mushrooms

Season the tofu with salt, white pepper and sansho pepper

three ways with dashi

SO ESSENTIAL IS DASHI BROTH TO JAPANESE COOKERY THAT IT IS OFTEN RIGHTFULLY CALLED THE SOUL OF JAPANESE CUISINE. FRAGRANT WITH THE AROMA OF THE SEA, IT DERIVES ITS RICH TASTE AND ESSENCE FROM KONBU (KELP) AND KATSUOBUSHI (DRIED BONITO FLAKES), ALTHOUGH A LIGHTER VEGETARIAN VERSION UTILIZES THE KELP ALONE. DASHI FORMS THE BASE OF MANY JAPANESE SOUPS, IS USED TO SIMMER VEGETABLES AND DILUTES AND FLAVOURS DRESSINGS. INSTANT DASHI GRANULES CAN BE A TIME-SAVING SUBSTITUTE.

dashi I

Wipe a 10 cm (4 in) square piece of konbu (kelp) with a damp cloth but do not rub off the white powdery substance that will become obvious as it dries. Cut the konbu into strips. Put the konbu and 1.5 litres (52 fl oz/6 cups) cold water into a saucepan and slowly bring to the boil, then remove the konbu. Quickly add 60 ml (2 fl oz/$1/4$ cup) cold water to stop the boiling process. Add 20 g ($3/4$ oz/ 1 cup) katsuobushi (bonito flakes), then return to the boil. Remove from the heat. Allow the katsuobushi to sink to the bottom of the pan, then strain the liquid through a fine sieve. The stock is now ready for making clear soups. Makes about 1 litre (35 fl oz/4 cups).

dashi II

Wipe a 10 cm (4 in) square piece of konbu (kelp) with a damp cloth but do not rub off the white powdery substance that will become obvious as it dries. Cut the konbu into strips. Put the konbu and 1.5 litres (52 fl oz/6 cups) cold water into a saucepan and slowly bring to the boil. Quickly add 60 ml (2 fl oz/$1/4$ cup) cold water to stop the boiling process. Add 20 g ($3/4$ oz/1 cup) katsuobushi (bonito flakes), return to the boil, then reduce the heat and simmer for 15 minutes. Remove from the heat. Allow the katsuobushi to sink to the bottom of the pan, then strain the liquid through a fine sieve. The stock is now ready for stews and thick soups. Makes about 1 litre (35 fl oz/4 cups).

konbu dashi I and II

For konbu dashi I, cut a 15 cm (6 in) square piece of konbu (kelp) into strips and put in a saucepan with 1.5 litres (52 fl oz/6 cups) cold water. Bring to the boil, then remove the konbu. For konbu dashi II, leave the piece of konbu in the pan, reduce to a simmer and cook for a further 10 minutes. Makes about 1.25 litres (44 fl oz/5 cups).

chilled tofu with ginger and spring onion
.... serves 4

ALTHOUGH DELICIOUS AT ANY TIME, CHILLED TOFU MAKES AN ESPECIALLY SUITABLE STARTER IN THE HEAT OF SUMMER. ITS DELICATE FLAVOUR AND CREAMY TEXTURE ARE WELL ACCENTED BY THE AROMATIC SHREDDED SHISO LEAVES, NUTTY SESAME SEEDS AND THE SAVOUR OF SOY SAUCE.

silken firm tofu	600 g (1 lb 5 oz) block, chilled
fresh ginger	1 tablespoon finely grated, and its juice
spring onions (scallions)	2, thinly sliced
white or black sesame seeds	2 teaspoons, toasted
shiso leaves	finely shredded, to garnish, optional
fine katsuobushi (bonito flakes)	to garnish, optional
shoyu (Japanese soy sauce)	for drizzling
sesame oil or chilli sesame oil	for drizzling

Be very careful when working with the tofu — it is very soft and breaks easily. Cut the tofu into quarters, then place one piece of tofu in each of four small serving bowls.

Top each serving with a little grated ginger and juice, some spring onion and sesame seeds. If you like, sprinkle the tofu with some shredded shiso leaves and katsuobushi. Drizzle with a little shoyu and sesame oil and serve immediately.

Tofu, introduced from China as a major dietary component of Zen Buddhist vegetarianism, has been eaten in Japan for nearly a thousand years. Made by soaking, crushing and boiling soya beans, the soya milk is squeezed out, strained and coagulated in moulds. This bean curd is a staple in Japanese cuisine, and is available in a delicate silken form, almost like custard, as well as a firmer 'cotton' variety. It is popularly eaten fresh, either warm in winter or chilled in summer, with soy sauce and other condiments. Cubes of tofu are added to miso soup, hotpot meals and stir-fried dishes, while thinly sliced and deep-fried, tofu makes tasty wrappers for rice.

miso ramen..serves 4

MISO RAMEN COMBINES TWO FAVOURITE JAPANESE TASTES — WHEAT NOODLES AND A DASHI–MISO BROTH, LIKE THAT USED TO MAKE THE BELOVED DAILY MISO SOUP. THIS FILLING MEAL IN A BOWL, SUPPLEMENTED WITH CUBES OF PROTEIN-RICH TOFU, IS A VEGETARIAN'S DELIGHT.

dried wakame seaweed pieces	2 teaspoons finely chopped
fresh ramen noodles	500 g (1 lb 2 oz)
silken firm tofu	200 g (7 oz), cut into 1.5 cm (5/8 in) cubes
spring onions (scallions)	2, thinly sliced on the diagonal
dashi II	1.5 litres (52 fl oz/6 cups) (see recipe on page 24)
red miso paste	2 tablespoons
white miso paste	1 tablespoon
mirin	1 tablespoon
shoyu (Japanese soy sauce)	3 teaspoons

Soak the wakame in cold water for 5 minutes, or until rehydrated and glossy but not mushy. Drain well and set aside.

Bring a large saucepan of lightly salted water to the boil, add the noodles and separate with chopsticks. Cook for 1–2 minutes, or until tender. Drain well, then rinse under cold running water, lightly rubbing the noodles together with your hands to remove any excess starch. Divide the noodles among four deep, warmed bowls. Top with the cubes of tofu and the spring onion.

Meanwhile, bring the dashi to the boil in a large saucepan, then reduce to a simmer.

Combine the red and white miso with 250 ml (9 fl oz/1 cup) of the dashi in a bowl. Whisk until smooth. Return the miso mixture to the saucepan and stir until combined. Bring the liquid just to the boil, then add the mirin, shoyu and wakame and gently heat for 1 minute. Stir, then ladle the broth over the ramen noodles, tofu and spring onion and serve immediately.

Soak the wakame in cold water until rehydrated

Add the ramen to boiling water and separate with chopsticks

Combine the miso with some of the dashi and stir until smooth

nabeyaki udon . . . . serves 4

FEATURING AN ABUNDANCE OF WONDERFUL FLAVOURS IN ITS VARIED TOPPINGS, THIS SOUP IS COOKED AND THEN SERVED IN FLAMEPROOF COVERED BOWLS. THE FINISHING TOUCH IS THE EGG NESTLED ON TOP — 'LIKE A MOON', AS THE JAPANESE SAY — WHICH IS POACHED IN THE BUBBLING BROTH.

dried shiitake mushrooms	4
sugar	1 teaspoon
dashi II	1 litre (35 fl oz/4 cups) (see recipe on page 24)
shoyu (Japanese soy sauce)	150 ml (5 fl oz)
mirin	70 ml (2¼ fl oz)
fresh udon noodles	750 g (1 lb 10 oz)
boneless, skinless chicken thighs	2, cut into bite-sized pieces
kamaboko (fish-paste loaf)	8 slices, 5 mm (¼ in) thick
spring onions (scallions)	2, sliced on the diagonal
eggs	4
tempura prawns (shrimp)	4, optional (see recipe on page 157)
shichimi togarashi (seven-spice mix)	to serve

Soak the shiitake in hot water for 30 minutes, then drain well. Discard the stems. Combine the sugar, 125 ml (4 fl oz/½ cup) of the dashi and 1 tablespoon each of the shoyu and mirin and bring to the boil. Add the shiitake and cook for 15 minutes, or until the liquid has almost been absorbed. Set the shiitake aside.

Bring a large saucepan of lightly salted water to the boil, add the noodles and cook for 5 minutes, stirring gently. Drain well and rinse. Divide the noodles among four 400 ml (14 fl oz) flameproof casserole dishes or claypots with lids. Combine the remaining dashi, shoyu and mirin in a saucepan with ½ teaspoon salt and bring to the boil, then pour the liquid over the noodles so that it just covers them.

Arrange a quarter of the shiitake, chicken, kamaboko and spring onion on top of the noodles in each dish, keeping each ingredient separate and leaving some clear space for the egg. Place each dish over medium–high heat (you may prefer to cook one or two at a time) and bring to the boil. Remove any scum that forms on the surface, then reduce to a simmer and cook for 7 minutes, or until the chicken is just cooked through. Turn off the heat.

Carefully crack an egg into a cup. Using a ladle, press a hollow into the clear space you left when arranging the ingredients, then carefully slide the raw egg into the hollow, without breaking the yolk. Repeat with the remaining eggs and dishes. Place the lids on top and set aside for 7 minutes, or until the egg is set. If there is a risk of salmonella in your area, leave the dishes on the heat until the egg is completely cooked through. If you like, serve with a tempura prawn on the side. Pass around the shichimi togarashi for sprinkling.

Soak the dried shiitake in hot water for 30 minutes

Cook the shiitake in the dashi mixture, stirring occasionally

udon noodle soup .... serves 4

FOR THOSE WHO LOVE THE FLAVOUR AND TEXTURE OF UDON NOODLES, THIS QUICK AND EASY BROTH IS MADE WITH INSTANT DASHI GRANULES. THE NOODLES MUST NOT BE OVERCOOKED, AS THEY SHOULD RETAIN SOME SUBSTANCE — WHAT THE JAPANESE CALL *KOSHI*.

dried udon noodles	400 g (14 oz)
dashi granules	3 teaspoons
leeks	2, white and pale green parts, washed well and cut into very thin slices
pork loin	200 g (7 oz), cut into thin strips
shoyu (Japanese soy sauce)	125 ml (4 fl oz/1/2 cup)
mirin	2 tablespoons
spring onions (scallions)	3, 2 cut into 4 cm (11/2 in) lengths, 1 finely chopped
shichimi togarashi (seven-spice mix)	to serve

Cook the noodles in a large saucepan of rapidly boiling water for 5 minutes, or until tender. Drain and cover to keep warm.

Combine 1 litre (35 fl oz/4 cups) water and the dashi granules in a large pan and bring to the boil. Add the leeks, then reduce the heat and simmer for 5 minutes. Add the pork, shoyu, mirin and lengths of spring onion and simmer for 2 minutes, or until the pork is cooked.

Divide the noodles among four serving bowls and ladle the soup over the top. Garnish with the chopped spring onion and sprinkle the shichimi togarashi over the top.

Shichimi togarashi, meaning 'seven-flavour hot red pepper', is a blend of *togarashi* pepper with at least six other spices. The ingredients and their proportions vary by region, maker and individual preferences. Typically the mix can contain any of the following: black or white sesame seeds, ground *sansho* pods, poppy seeds, mustard, hemp seeds, rape seeds, nori flakes, and sometimes *chinpi*, the dried peel of citron, bitter orange or tangerine. Although available in any supermarket in Japan, it is a favourite souvenir item among Japanese, purchased at spice shops while visiting old Kyoto or other famous tourist sites. The spice mix is sprinkled on soups, noodles and meat dishes.

ramen noodles with soy broth

RAMEN ARE CHINESE WHEAT NOODLES, EATEN IN JAPAN SINCE THE 17TH CENTURY. SERVED IN A CLEAR BROWN BROTH PREPARED FROM PORK AND CHICKEN BONES, FLAVOURED WITH SOY SAUCE AND TOPPED WITH SLICED PORK AND VEGETABLES, IT MAKES A COMPLETE SOUP MEAL.

broth

pork bones	1 kg (2 lb 4 oz)
chicken bones	1 kg (2 lb 4 oz)
spring onions (scallions)	10, bruised
fresh ginger	10 cm (4 in) piece, sliced
garlic	1 bulb, cut in half through the centre
carrots	2, peeled and chopped
konbu (kelp)	10 cm (4 in) square piece, wiped with a damp cloth
shoyu (Japanese soy sauce)	125–185 ml (4–6 fl oz/1/2–3/4 cup)
sake	80 ml (21/2 fl oz/1/3 cup)
dried shiitake mushrooms	8
fresh ramen noodles	500 g (1 lb 2 oz)
bamboo shoots	100 g (31/2 oz), sliced
Chinese barbecued pork	125 g (41/2 oz), sliced
bok choy (pak choy)	200 g (7 oz), sliced lengthways into wide strips, blanched
bean sprouts	50 g (13/4 oz), blanched
spring onions (scallions)	4, cut into 4 cm (11/2 in) lengths
shichimi togarashi (seven-spice mix)	to serve, optional
chilli sesame oil	to serve, optional

To make the broth, put the pork and chicken bones in a stockpot or large, deep saucepan and cover with cold water. Bring to the boil over high heat, then drain. Rinse the bones, then return them to a clean stockpot. Add the spring onions, ginger, garlic, carrot and konbu and pour in enough cold water to cover by about 5 cm (2 in). Bring to the boil over high heat, remove the konbu, then reduce to a simmer, skimming any scum off the surface. Cook, uncovered, for 6 hours, or until the liquid has reduced to about 1.5 litres (52 fl oz/6 cups). Cool slightly, remove the bones, then pour the stock through a fine strainer. Refrigerate for 6 hours, or until cold.

Meanwhile, soak the shiitake in hot water for 30 minutes, then drain well. Discard the stems.

Bring a large saucepan of lightly salted water to the boil, add the noodles and separate with chopsticks. Cook for 1–2 minutes, or until tender. Drain well, then rinse under cold running water, rubbing the noodles together lightly with your hands to remove any excess starch.

Scoop off any fat from the surface of the cooled broth, then pour the broth into a large saucepan. Add the shoyu and sake, bring to the boil over high heat, then reduce to a simmer. Pour a little broth into four large warmed bowls, then divide the noodles among the bowls. Ladle the broth over the noodles so that it just comes to the top of the noodles. Using chopsticks, neatly arrange small piles of the shiitake, bamboo shoots, pork, bok choy, bean sprouts and spring onion on top of the noodles. If you like, sprinkle with shichimi togarashi and drizzle with a little chilli sesame oil. Freeze any leftover broth for next time.

perfect miso soup

One of the most important ingredients in Japanese cooking is miso, a rich, earthy paste made from fermented soya beans. The soya beans are boiled and then ground into a thick paste, with added wheat, barley or rice. This paste is then injected with a yeast and left to ferment. There are many different grades and colours of miso, each suited to a particular recipe. Generally the lighter the colour, the sweeter and less salty the taste. *Shiro miso*, or 'white miso', is actually closer to yellow in colour and has a mild flavour; *shinshu miso* is an all-purpose yellowish miso; *aka miso*, meaning 'red miso', is a deep red, almost caramel colour; and the strongly flavoured, salty *hatcho miso* is dark reddish-brown and should be used sparingly — don't confuse it with red miso.

To make miso soup, first soak 1½ teaspoons dried wakame seaweed pieces in cold water for 5 minutes, or until rehydrated and glossy. Drain well, then divide among four small soup bowls. Cut 200 g (7 oz) silken firm tofu into 1.5 cm (⅝ in) cubes and thinly slice 1 spring onion (scallion). Divide the tofu and spring onion among the bowls.

Pour 875 ml (30 fl oz/3½ cups) dashi II or konbu dashi II (see recipes on page 24) into a saucepan and bring to the boil. Combine 100 g (3½ oz/⅓ cup) red or white miso paste (or a mixture of both) with 250 ml (9 fl oz/1 cup) of the dashi stock in a bowl. Whisk until smooth. Return the miso mixture to the saucepan and stir until combined — be careful not to boil the broth as this will diminish the flavour of the miso. Ladle into the bowls until they are two-thirds full and serve immediately. To drink the miso, sip the soup from the bowl by resting the bowl in your left hand and tilting it to your lips with your right hand. You can use chopsticks to eat the solid ingredients. Serves 4 as a starter

seafood and vegetable fritters... serves 6–8

HERE, QUANTITIES OF CHOPPED SEAFOOD AND VEGETABLES ARE TOSSED TOGETHER WITH BATTER AND THEN DEEP-FRIED BY THE SPOONFUL. THE SECRET TO CRISPY–LIGHT FRITTERS IS TO HAVE THE FOOD AND BATTER AS COLD AS POSSIBLE AND TO MAKE THE BATTER JUST BEFORE YOU ARE READY TO USE IT.

raw prawns (shrimp)	300 g (10 1/2 oz), peeled, deveined
scallops	100 g (3 1/2 oz), roe removed
carrot	1 small, peeled
daikon	5 cm (2 in) piece (about 70 g/2 1/2 oz), peeled
onion	1 small
green beans	6
mitsuba or flat-leaf (Italian) parsley, with stems	2 large handfuls
plain (all-purpose) flour	1 1/2 tablespoons
vegetable oil	for deep-frying
sesame oil	60 ml (2 fl oz/1/4 cup)
tempura batter	1 quantity (see recipe on page 157)
tempura dipping sauce	1 quantity (see recipe on page 131), or ready-made

Chop the prawns and scallops into small pieces. Cut the carrot and daikon into 4 cm (1 1/2 in) lengths, then finely julienne, using a very sharp knife or Japanese mandolin with a medium-tooth blade. Cut the onion in half and thinly slice. Thinly slice the beans on the diagonal. Roughly chop the mitsuba leaves and stems.

Put the chopped seafood, julienned vegetables and chopped mitsuba in a bowl with the flour and mix to combine.

Fill a deep-fat fryer or large saucepan one-third full of vegetable oil, then add the sesame oil. Heat to 170°C (325°F), or until a cube of bread dropped into the oil browns in 20 seconds.

Make the tempura batter. Lightly mix the seafood and vegetable mixture through the tempura batter. Working in batches, drop heaped tablespoons of the mixture into the hot oil and cook for 3–4 minutes, or until crisp, golden and cooked through. Drain on paper towels and serve immediately with the dipping sauce.

Cut the daikon into short lengths, then julienne with a sharp knife

Add the flour to the seafood, vegetables and mitsuba

Mix the seafood and vegetables through the tempura batter

deep-fried marinated chicken . . . . serves 6–8

A TENDERIZING AND FLAVOUR ENHANCING MARINADE USES A TRIO OF JAPANESE-STYLE LIQUID SEASONINGS FOR THE CHICKEN — SOY SAUCE, MIRIN AND SAKE. THE ADDITION OF GINGER AND GARLIC TO THE BLEND ADDS A FURTHER FLAVOUR BOOST TO THESE DEEP-FRIED CHICKEN MORSELS.

chicken thigh cutlets	1 kg (2 lb 4 oz), skin on
shoyu (Japanese soy sauce)	60 ml (2 fl oz/¼ cup)
mirin	60 ml (2 fl oz/¼ cup)
sake	1 tablespoon
fresh ginger	2 teaspoons finely grated, and its juice
garlic	3 cloves, crushed
vegetable oil	for deep-frying
potato starch	for coating
lemon wedges	to serve

Remove the bones from the cutlets and cut the chicken into 4 cm (1½ in) squares. Combine the shoyu, mirin, sake, ginger and juice, and garlic in a non-metallic bowl and add the chicken. Stir to coat, cover with plastic wrap and marinate in the refrigerator for 1 hour.

Fill a deep-fat fryer or large saucepan one-third full of oil and heat to 180°C (350°F), or until a cube of bread dropped into the oil browns in 15 seconds.

Drain the chicken pieces well, discarding the marinade. Lightly coat the chicken with the potato starch and shake off any excess. Deep-fry in batches for 6–7 minutes, or until golden and crisp and the chicken is just cooked through. Drain well on paper towels and sprinkle with salt. Serve with lemon wedges.

Mirin is a popular seasoning and often the source of the slight sweetness common to so many Japanese dishes. The best of this cooking 'wine' is made from steamed glutinous rice (*mochi-gome*) that has begun to mould, and to which distilled spirits have then been added. Usually left to ferment and sweeten for up to 2 months, it develops an alcohol content of 12–15 per cent. The alcohol is often burned off during the cooking process. It is well worth seeking out *hon mirin*, the 'true' mirin, which is brewed in a slow and more costly traditional way, rather than choosing a cheaper substitute, which has been artificially flavoured and sweetened with sugar.

soba noodles in broth . . . . serves 4

BUCKWHEAT IS A FLAVOUR OF THE COUNTRYSIDE, AND JAPANESE WEEKEND TRAVELLERS OFTEN BRING PACKETS OF NOODLES BACK AS SOUVENIR GIFTS FOR FRIENDS AND RELATIVES. FILLING BUT NOT HEAVY, THIS SIMPLE, ALMOST SPARTAN, BOWL OF SOBA MAKES A GREAT SNACK OR RESTORATIVE SOUP.

dashi II	2 litres (70 fl oz/8 cups)
	(see recipe on page 24)
shoyu (Japanese soy sauce)	125 ml (4 fl oz/1/2 cup)
caster (superfine) sugar	1 1/2 tablespoons
mirin	2 tablespoons
dried soba (buckwheat) noodles	350 g (12 oz)
spring onions (scallions)	2, thinly sliced on the diagonal
shichimi togarashi	to serve, optional
(seven-spice mix)	

Combine the dashi and 1/2 teaspoon salt in a saucepan and bring to the boil over high heat. Add the shoyu, sugar and mirin and stir until the sugar dissolves. Bring to the boil, then reduce the heat and simmer for 20 minutes.

Meanwhile, half-fill a large saucepan with lightly salted water and bring to the boil over high heat, then gradually lower the noodles into the water. Stir so the noodles don't stick together. Pour in 250 ml (9 fl oz/1 cup) cold water and return to the boil. Repeat this step another two to three times, or until the noodles are tender. This cooking method helps to cook this delicate noodle more evenly. The noodles should be *al dente* with no hard core in the centre but not completely soft all the way through.

Drain the noodles, then rinse well under cold running water, lightly rubbing the noodles together with your hands to remove any excess starch.

Divide the noodles among four deep noodle bowls and ladle over the broth. Top with the spring onion and serve immediately. If you like, pass around the shichimi togarashi for sprinkling.

Gradually lower the soba noodles into the boiling water

Stir the noodles, then pour in cold water and return to the boil

When cooked, rinse the noodles under cold running water

tofu dengaku

JAPANESE HAVE A LONG TRADITION OF EATING MISO-TOPPED TOFU. THIS NUTRITIOUS DISH CAME TO BE CALLED *DENGAKU*, NAMED FOR THE WOODEN SKEWERS ON WHICH IT WAS SOMETIMES COOKED. THESE LONG SKEWERS WERE REMINISCENT OF THE STILTS WORN IN AN ANCIENT DANCE OF THE SAME NAME.

firm (cotton) tofu	700 g (1 lb 9 oz)
red or white miso paste	100 g (3½ oz/⅓ cup)
egg yolk	1
dashi II	1½ tablespoons
	(see recipe on page 24)
mirin	2 teaspoons
sugar	2 teaspoons
vegetable oil	for brushing
nori flakes	to garnish
spring onion (scallion)	thinly sliced, to garnish
sesame seeds	lightly toasted, to garnish

To weight the tofu, wrap it in a clean tea towel (dish towel). Put two plates on top of the tofu to extract any excess moisture and leave for 1 hour, or until the tofu is about half its original thickness. Remove from the tea towel and pat dry with paper towels.

Meanwhile, combine the miso, egg yolk, dashi, mirin and sugar in a bowl and whisk until smooth.

Preheat the grill (broiler) to high. Cut the tofu into six even slices and put on a foil-lined tray. Lightly brush the tofu blocks with a little vegetable oil and put under the grill for 2–3 minutes, or until lightly golden. Turn the tofu over and cook the other side.

Thickly spread the miso mixture onto one side of the tofu and sit under the grill again, miso side up, for a few minutes, or until bubbling and golden in places. Serve immediately, sprinkled with one or a mixture of the garnishes.

Miso, a fermented paste of soya beans, salt and often an added grain such as rice or barley, is a basic flavouring ingredient of the Japanese kitchen. Varying greatly by region, literally hundreds of varieties are produced across the country. Miso ranges in colour from creamy white to golden, and reddish brown to chocolate. Some are smooth and others chunky, some sweet and mild, while others are salty and pungent. Highly nutritious and versatile, miso comprises the base of Japan's traditional and indispensable daily soup. It also serves as a popular savoury marinade for fish or meat, is used in sauces and dressings, and sometimes as a dip.

japanese spring rolls..makes 12

SPRING ROLLS ORIGINATED LONG AGO IN CHINA AS A SPRING FESTIVAL FOOD, BUT ARE NOW POPULAR IN MANY ASIAN CUISINES, WITH AS MANY NATIONAL VARIATIONS. THE JAPANESE VERSION, CALLED *HARUMAKI*, ENCLOSE A FLAVOURFUL MEAT, VEGETABLE AND NOODLE FILLING.

dipping sauce

tamari or shoyu (Japanese soy sauce)	60 ml (2 fl oz/^{1}/4 cup)
Japanese rice vinegar	1 ^{1}/2 tablespoons
mirin	1 tablespoon
caster (superfine) sugar	1 teaspoon

filling

Chinese cabbage	90 g (3^1/4 oz), finely shredded
dried shiitake mushrooms	3
harusame (bean thread noodles)	30 g (1 oz)
minced (ground) pork	200 g (7 oz)
bamboo shoots	90 g (3^1/4 oz), finely chopped
spring onions (scallions)	4, finely chopped
fresh ginger	1 tablespoon finely grated
garlic	1 clove, crushed
sake	1 ^{1}/2 tablespoons
shoyu (Japanese soy sauce)	1 ^{1}/2 tablespoons
mirin	1 tablespoon
sesame oil	1 teaspoon
ground white pepper	large pinch
potato starch	2 tablespoons, plus 1 tablespoon extra
spring roll wrappers	12, 18 cm (7 in) square
vegetable oil	for deep-frying

To make the dipping sauce, combine all the ingredients in a small bowl and stir until the sugar has dissolved.

To make the filling, put the cabbage in a colander. Sprinkle with salt and set aside for 30 minutes, then squeeze well. Meanwhile, soak the shiitake in hot water for 30 minutes. Drain, discard the stems and thinly slice the caps. Soak the harusame in warm water for 10 minutes. Drain, squeeze out any excess moisture, then roughly chop. Put the cabbage, shiitake and noodles in a large bowl with the rest of the filling ingredients except the potato starch and mix well. Add the potato starch and mix again. Season with salt.

Combine the extra potato starch with enough cold water to form a thin paste. Lay a spring roll wrapper on a work surface with one corner of the wrapper facing you. Put 1 heaped tablespoon of the filling in a sausage shape across the wrapper, about 2 cm (^{3}/4 in) up from the bottom corner. Fold the bottom corner over and roll up, folding in the sides as you go. Seal the edge with a little of the potato starch paste. Set aside and continue with the remaining wrappers and filling.

Fill a deep-fat fryer or large saucepan one-third full of oil and heat to 170°C (325°F), or until a cube of bread dropped into the oil browns in 20 seconds. Fry the spring rolls a few at a time for 10 minutes, or until golden and cooked through. Drain on paper towels and keep warm in a low oven while you cook the rest. Serve immediately with the dipping sauce.

sides and salads

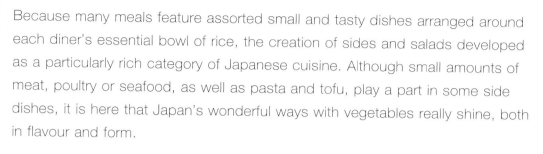

Because many meals feature assorted small and tasty dishes arranged around each diner's essential bowl of rice, the creation of sides and salads developed as a particularly rich category of Japanese cuisine. Although small amounts of meat, poultry or seafood, as well as pasta and tofu, play a part in some side dishes, it is here that Japan's wonderful ways with vegetables really shine, both in flavour and form.

A great number of these would be categorized as *nimono*, simmered dishes. Prepared in a little dashi, they can be further seasoned with sake, mirin and soy sauce, and possibly flavourful miso, ginger or sesame seeds. Ingredients are cut in ways to provide visual interest — cut on the diagonal or in cubes with the edges bevelled, or even with pieces of skin left unpeeled to provide colour contrast. They are typically served in attractive mounds in vessels that have been carefully selected to reflect the season and enhance the contents. Often served at room temperature, many side dishes can be prepared a little in advance for convenience.

Japanese salads are quite different from Western salads, and the deep crunchiness we often associate with salads is absent. Briny sea plants may be combined with vegetables, which are not often completely raw but instead have been salted, blanched or parboiled, making them slightly soft but still with an appealing bite to their texture. They may be classified as either *sunomono*, vinegared things, or *aemono*, dressed things.

Vinegared salads have a very light and fresh taste. Rice vinegar is commonly used, and is diluted not with oil but with the incredibly versatile dashi. This Japanese-style vinaigrette may be sweetened with mirin or sugar and flavoured with either a light or dark soy sauce. Dressed salads tend to be somewhat more full bodied, sometimes utilizing a mayonnaise dressing or some other creamy mixture calling for tofu, miso, ground seeds or nuts to give richness.

For grinding the frequently-called-for sesame seeds, as well as many other ingredients, a Japanese-style *suribachi* and *surikogi*, a clay mortar and wooden pestle, are very handy, and produce the desired authentic texture. When the mortar is used to blend a dressing, the salad might be tossed and brought to the table in the mortar, which doubles as a serving bowl.

beans with sesame miso dressing

serves 4–6

INGEN, OR GREEN BEANS, ARE NAMED AFTER THE CHINESE BUDDHIST PRIEST WHO IS SAID TO HAVE INTRODUCED THEM INTO JAPAN SEVERAL CENTURIES AGO. THEIR FRESH, SLIGHTLY CRISP TASTE IS COMPLEMENTED HERE BY THE CREAMY, SOMEWHAT NUTTY FLAVOUR OF THE DRESSING.

green beans	250 g (9 oz), trimmed and cut into 5 cm (2 in) lengths

dressing

sesame seeds	50 g (1¾ oz/⅓ cup)
sugar	1 teaspoon
red or white miso paste	2 tablespoons
mirin	2 tablespoons

Bring a saucepan of lightly salted water to the boil. Add the beans and cook for 2 minutes, or until just tender. Drain, plunge into iced water until cool, then drain well.

To make the dressing, dry-fry the sesame seeds over medium heat, stirring regularly, for 5 minutes, or until lightly golden and aromatic. Immediately scoop the sesame seeds into a mortar or a suribachi (Japanese ribbed mortar), reserving 1 teaspoon of whole seeds for the garnish, and grind with a pestle until very finely crushed. Gradually incorporate the sugar, miso and mirin to form a thickish paste.

Put the beans in a bowl with the dressing and toss to combine. Serve in a mound in a bowl or on a plate and sprinkle with the reserved sesame seeds.

Black, white or golden in colour, sesame seeds, goma, are used to add a nutty flavour and aroma to many dishes. They are lightly toasted and used as a garnish, either crushed or whole, on noodles and vegetables, and sometimes are pressed onto rice crackers to lend extra flavour and texture. Crushed or puréed, they are added to savoury dressings and dips. Sesame paste is occasionally used in traditional and contemporary Japanese sweets. Oil is also pressed from the oil-rich white seeds. A little sesame oil is often added to less expensive and more neutral tasting oils to impart its distinctive flavour to certain fried foods, most particularly tempura.

crab, cucumber and wakame salad

THIS APPEALINGLY FRESH SUMMER SALAD COMBINES THREE CONTRASTING TEXTURES OF CRAB, CUCUMBER AND SEAWEED. THE LIGHT DRESSING, WHICH, LIKE MOST JAPANESE DRESSINGS, DILUTES THE VINEGAR WITH DASHI RATHER THAN OIL, ENHANCES THE NATURAL FLAVOURS OF THE INGREDIENTS WHILE NEVER OVERPOWERING THEM.

Lebanese (short) cucumbers	2
dried wakame seaweed pieces	2 tablespoons
crabmeat	150 g (5½ oz/1 cup) fresh, cooked, picked over (or good-quality tinned crabmeat)

dressing

Japanese rice vinegar	2 tablespoons
dashi II	2 tablespoons (see recipe on page 24)
shoyu (Japanese soy sauce)	1 tablespoon
mirin	2 teaspoons
fresh ginger	20 g (¾ oz)

Dissolve 2 teaspoons salt in 500 ml (17 fl oz/2 cups) cold water. Cut the cucumbers in half lengthways, scoop out the seeds, then slice the flesh very thinly. Put the cucumber flesh in the cold water and soak for 10 minutes. Drain well and squeeze out any excess moisture. Keep in the refrigerator until needed.

Soak the wakame in a bowl of cold water for 5 minutes, or until rehydrated and glossy but not mushy. Drain well, then refrigerate until needed.

To make the dressing, combine the rice vinegar, dashi, shoyu and mirin in a small saucepan and bring to the boil over high heat. Remove from the heat and cool to room temperature. Finely grate the ginger, then squeeze the grated ginger with your fingertips to release the juice (you will need 1½ teaspoons of ginger juice). Add the ginger juice to the dressing and stir well. Allow to cool completely. Refrigerate for 15 minutes, or until cold.

Neatly arrange the cucumber, wakame and crabmeat in four small serving dishes, then carefully pour the dressing over the top.

Halve the cucumbers lengthways, scoop out the seeds and slice

Soak the cucumber slices in cold salted water for 10 minutes

Drain the cucumbers, then squeeze out the excess moisture

white salad . . . . serves 6–8

HIGH IN FIBRE AND WITH NO FAT, KONNYAKU (OR YAM CAKE) ADDS ITS UNIQUE CHEWY TEXTURE TO A SIMMERED VEGETABLE ASSORTMENT BURSTING WITH NUTRITION. THIS DISH IS CALLED 'WHITE SALAD' FOR ITS CREAMY BUT LIGHT TOFU-BASED DRESSING, AND GROUND TOASTED SESAME SEEDS GIVE IT A DISTINCTIVE NUTTY FLAVOUR.

tofu dressing

silken firm tofu	200 g (7 oz)
sesame seeds	50 g (1^3/$_4$ oz/^{1}/$_3$ cup), toasted
caster (superfine) sugar	1 tablespoon
white miso paste	1 tablespoon
dashi II	1 tablespoon
	(see recipe on page 24)
shoyu (Japanese soy sauce)	2 teaspoons
mirin	3 teaspoons
sake	3 teaspoons

salad

konnyaku (yam cake)	100 g (3^1/$_2$ oz)
carrot	1 small, peeled
dashi II	170 ml (5^1/$_2$ fl oz/^{2}/$_3$ cup)
	(see recipe on page 24)
shoyu (Japanese soy sauce)	3 teaspoons
mirin	1 tablespoon
baby green beans	12, cut into 3 cm (1^1/$_4$ in) lengths
fresh shiitake mushrooms	6, stems discarded, caps sliced

To weight the tofu, first wrap it in a clean tea towel (dish towel). Put two plates on top of the tofu and leave for about 2 hours to extract any excess moisture.

Meanwhile, prepare the salad. Boil the konnyaku for 2 minutes, then cut into 3 cm x 5 mm (1^1/$_4$ x ^{1}/$_4$ in) strips. Cut the carrot into 5 cm (2 in) long pieces. Slice each piece into thin, 1 cm (^{1}/$_2$ in) wide batons.

Combine the dashi, shoyu and mirin in a saucepan and bring to the boil over high heat. Reduce to a simmer, then add the konnyaku, carrot and beans and cook for 3 minutes, or until the carrot is tender. Remove the vegetables with a slotted spoon and set aside. Add the shiitake to the pan, increase the heat to high and cook for 1–2 minutes, or until the liquid has almost evaporated. Cool completely.

Remove the tofu from the tea towel, then pat dry with paper towels. Finely mash the tofu with the back of a fork and set aside.

To make the dressing, grind the sesame seeds using a mortar and pestle or a *suribachi* (Japanese ribbed mortar) until finely crushed. Gradually mix in the sugar, miso, dashi, shoyu, mirin and sake until smooth. Stir the mashed tofu into the mixture.

Put the cooled carrot and shiitake mixtures in a bowl with the dressing and toss to combine. Serve in a neat mound in a large serving bowl or in small individual dishes.

shiitake with ponzu dressing

THESE SHIITAKE CAPS ARE ONLY LIGHTLY SAUTEED SO THEY RETAIN THEIR FORM AND FLESHY SUBSTANCE. THE CITRUSY PONZU SAUCE CREATES A BRILLIANT COUNTERPOINT TO THE WOODSY AROMA THE MUSHROOMS EXUDE. THE OPTIONAL SESAME OIL CAN ADD YET ANOTHER FLAVOUR DIMENSION.

fresh shiitake mushrooms	200 g (7 oz)
vegetable oil	1 tablespoon
ponzu	60 ml (2 fl oz/¼ cup), ready-made or see recipe on page 131
sesame oil	to serve, optional

Remove the stems from the shiitake and discard them. Cut any larger caps in half.

Heat the oil in a frying pan over medium–high heat, add the shiitake and season with salt. Cook the mushrooms for 2 minutes on each side, or until tender. Transfer to a shallow bowl and pour over the ponzu. Drizzle with a little sesame oil if desired.

Ponzu is made from the juice of a citrus fruit, such as bitter orange, citron, lemon or several distinctly Japanese citrus varieties. Japanese dictionaries credit 17th-century Dutch visitors for the origin of this word, adopted from the Dutch word *pons*, a word then apparently in use to mean citrus, and -*zu* (from *su*), which means vinegar in Japanese. In recent years *ponzu-joyu*, a blend of ponzu and soy sauce, further seasoned with splashes of mirin and dashi broth, has become popular at the table. Used as a dipping sauce, it adds a piquant touch to raw shellfish, particularly oysters on the half-shell, and a variety of chicken or fish-and-vegetable hotpots.

japanese potato salad .... serves 6–8

THIS INTERESTINGLY TEXTURED POTATO SALAD BEGINS WITH LIGHTLY CRUSHED POTATOES INSTEAD OF THE MORE USUAL CHUNKS, WITH CRUNCHY CUCUMBERS AND SLIVERS OF TENDER HAM ADDED IN. A MAYONNAISE DRESSING SEASONED WITH ONIONS AND MITSUBA MELDS IT TOGETHER.

all-purpose potatoes	500 g (1 lb 2 oz), peeled
sliced ham	50 g (1³/4 oz)
Lebanese (short) cucumber	1

dressing

Japanese mayonnaise	185 g (6¹/2 oz/³/4 cup)
Japanese mustard	1/2 teaspoon
Japanese rice vinegar	2 tablespoons
sesame oil	a few drops
spring onions (scallions)	2, finely chopped
mitsuba or flat-leaf (Italian) parsley	2 large handfuls, finely chopped, plus extra leaves to garnish, optional
ground white pepper	to season

Cut the potatoes into 2 cm (³/4 in) dice. Bring a saucepan of salted water to the boil and add the potato. Cook for 8 minutes, or until tender. Drain, rinse under cold running water, then drain again. Lightly crush the potatoes with a fork but do not mash them — there should still be some lumps.

Meanwhile, cut the ham into thin strips, about 3 cm (1¹/4 in) in length. Cut the cucumber in half lengthways and scoop out the seeds with a teaspoon, then slice very thinly.

To make the dressing, combine the mayonnaise, mustard, vinegar and sesame oil in a bowl. Mix until smooth, then stir in the spring onion and mitsuba. Season with salt and white pepper.

Put the warm potato, ham, cucumber and dressing in a bowl and toss to combine well. Set aside for 15 minutes so the potato can absorb some of the dressing and the flavours can develop. Serve in a bowl garnished with extra mitsuba leaves, if desired.

Lightly crush the potatoes with a fork but do not mash them

Combine the mayonnaise, mustard, vinegar and sesame oil

Stir in the spring onion and chopped mitsuba

three ways with daikon

THE APPEARANCE OF THIS LONG WHITE DAIKON RADISH, ITS NAME MEANING 'BIG ROOT', SOMEWHAT BELIES THE GREAT INTEREST IT AROUSES ON THE JAPANESE TABLE. THIS POPULAR VEGETABLE CAN HAVE A FLAVOUR RANGING FROM MILD TO A BIT SPICY, AND IS PREPARED IN A GREAT VARIETY OF WAYS. RAW, IT IS DELICIOUS IN SALADS, AS AN 'ANGEL HAIR' JULIENNE BENEATH SASHIMI, OR GRATED AS A CONDIMENT. IT IS OFTEN SIMMERED OR BRAISED, AND EVEN ITS GREEN TOPS ARE USEFUL AND TASTY, ADDED TO SOUP OR PICKLED IN BRINE.

simmered daikon

Peel 600 g (1 lb 5 oz) daikon (1 small daikon) and cut into 3 cm (1¼ in) thick slices. Soften the edges by running a sharp knife or vegetable peeler along the sharp edges so the shape is slightly rounded — this helps the daikon to retain its shape when cooked. Cut a shallow cross on one of the flat sides of each daikon. Put the daikon, cross side down, in a large saucepan. Cover generously with water and bring to the boil, then reduce the heat and simmer for 45 minutes, or until translucent. Drain the daikon. Combine 625 ml (21½ fl oz/2½ cups) dashi II (see recipe on page 24), 2 tablespoons shoyu (Japanese soy sauce), 1 tablespoon mirin, 2 teaspoons sugar and a 5 cm (2 in) square piece of konbu (kelp), wiped with a damp cloth, in a clean saucepan and bring to the boil, stirring until the sugar has dissolved. Add the daikon and bring just to the boil again. Reduce to a simmer, cover and cook for 30 minutes, or until the daikon is soft but not breaking up. To serve, put the konbu in the base of a shallow bowl, stack the daikon on top and ladle over a little sauce. Serves 4–6 as a side.

daikon and carrot salad

Peel 200 g (7 oz) daikon (about one-third of a small daikon) and 1 carrot, then cut both into 5 cm (2 in) lengths. Very finely julienne both, either by using a Japanese mandolin with the medium-tooth blade or by very thinly slicing the lengths and then cutting these slices into very thin strips. Put the julienned vegetables in a colander and sprinkle with salt. Set aside for 30 minutes, then rinse and drain well, squeezing out any excess moisture. Meanwhile, to make the dressing combine 80 ml (2½ fl oz/⅓ cup) Japanese rice vinegar with 2 tablespoons caster (superfine) sugar and ¼ teaspoon salt and stir until the sugar and salt have dissolved. Transfer the daikon and carrot mixture to a non-metallic bowl. Wipe a 4 cm (1½ in) square piece of konbu (kelp) with a damp cloth, cut into 1 cm (½ in) wide strips and add to the daikon and carrot. Pour over the dressing and stir. Cover with plastic wrap and refrigerate for 24–48 hours, stirring occasionally. When ready to serve, discard the konbu. Drain the vegetables. Scoop into a serving dish and, if you like, sprinkle with 1 teaspoon black sesame seeds. This is a good accompaniment to fried foods. Serves 6–8 as a side.

daikon with soba noodles and wakame

Cook 200 g (7 oz) peeled and grated daikon in a frying pan with 1 tablespoon vegetable oil for 5 minutes, stirring until the daikon begins to turn golden. Put in a bowl and cool. Put 10 g (¼ oz) dried wakame seaweed in a bowl and cover with cold water for 10 minutes, then drain and chop. Add to the daikon with 3 thinly sliced spring onions (scallions). Cook 200 g (7 oz) dried soba (buckwheat) noodles in 2 litres (70 fl oz/8 cups) boiling water for 2 minutes. Drain, rinse with cold water and drain again. Add to the daikon mixture. Combine 2 teaspoons dashi granules in a bowl with 2 tablespoons hot water. Stir in 1 teaspoon sugar, 2 teaspoons sesame oil, 2 tablespoons shoyu (Japanese soy sauce), 1 tablespoon mirin and 2 teaspoons finely grated fresh ginger. Pour over the noodle mixture and toss well to combine. Sprinkle with 2 teaspoons lightly toasted sesame seeds. Serves 4 as a starter.

simmered daikon

scallop and spinach salad .... serves 4

COOKING THE SCALLOPS FOR A SHORT TIME WILL ENSURE THEY WILL BE A MOIST AND TENDER CENTREPIECE TO THIS SALAD. THE DRESSING BLENDS WONDERFUL FLAVOURS, FROM THE PIQUANCY OF LIME JUICE, TO THE SALTINESS OF FISH SAUCE AND THE CARAMEL SWEETNESS OF PALM SUGAR.

scallops	300 g (10½ oz), roe removed
baby English spinach	100 g (3½ oz/2 cups) leaves
red capsicum (pepper)	1 small, cut into thin strips
bean sprouts	50 g (1¾ oz)
black sesame seeds	toasted, to garnish

dressing

sake	1½ tablespoons
lime juice	1 tablespoon
palm sugar (jaggery)	2 teaspoons shaved
fish sauce	1 teaspoon

Remove any veins, membrane or hard white muscle from the scallops. Lightly brush a chargrill pan or plate with oil and cook the scallops in batches for 1 minute on each side, or until cooked.

Divide the spinach leaves, capsicum and bean sprouts among four serving plates. Arrange the scallops over the top.

To make the dressing, whisk together the sake, lime juice, palm sugar and fish sauce. Pour over the salad, sprinkle with toasted sesame seeds and serve immediately.

Scallops, or *hotate-gai*, thrive in cold, clean waters such as those off the coast of Hokkaido, Japan's northernmost island, and northern Honshu. Besides harvesting wild scallops from the sea bottom, the Japanese have also successfully engaged in large-scale farming of these shellfish for some decades. The tender and delicately flavoured flesh is highly appreciated raw as sashimi. It is a popular ingredient in seafood hotpots, *nabe*, can be prepared teriyaki-style, or cooked on the half-shell with a touch of added sake or butter.

pumpkin with pickled plum dressing

A PICKLED PLUM DRESSING AND SHISO GARNISH MAKE LIVELY FLAVOUR CONTRASTS WITH THE SWEET PUMPKIN (WINTER SQUASH). THE PUMPKIN SKIN IS ONLY PARTIALLY PARED AWAY, WHILE BEVELLING AROUND THE EDGES ASSURES EVEN COOKING AND MORE SURFACE TO HOLD THE DRESSING.

dressing

umeboshi (pickled plums)	5 small (about 40 g /1 1/2 oz total) or 1 1/2–2 tablespoons pickled plum purée
shoyu (Japanese soy sauce)	2 teaspoons
mirin	1 tablespoon
dashi II	2 tablespoons (see recipe on page 24)
caster (superfine) sugar	1/4 teaspoon
jap or kent pumpkin (winter squash)	500 g (1 lb 2 oz), unpeeled and seeded
shiso leaves	2 teaspoons very finely shredded, or 1 thinly sliced spring onion (scallion)

To make the dressing, if you are using umeboshi, prick them all over with a fork, then soak in cold water for 2 hours, changing the water occasionally — this helps remove the excess salt. Drain and pat dry with paper towels, then remove the seeds and purée the flesh in a food processor or push through a fine sieve. Put the puréed umeboshi or ready-made purée in a small bowl along with the remaining dressing ingredients and stir well to combine.

Cut the pumpkin into 4 cm (1 1/2 in) cubes. Peel just around the edges of the skin on each piece, then run a knife or vegetable peeler along the sharp edges so the cube shape is softened and slightly rounded.

Bring a saucepan of lightly salted water to the boil, add the pumpkin and cook for 10–12 minutes, or until tender but not mushy. Drain well and set aside to cool to room temperature.

Lightly toss the cooled pumpkin with the dressing, then pile neatly into a serving dish. Sprinkle with the finely sliced shiso leaves or spring onion.

Prick the umeboshi with a fork before soaking in cold water

Stir the dressing ingredients into the puréed umeboshi

Slice off the sharp edges of the pumpkin cubes

somen noodle, prawn and cucumber salad

SOMEN NOODLES, QUICKLY COOKED AND REFRESHED IN COLD WATER, ARE A SUMMER FAVOURITE IN JAPAN. HERE THEY ARE HAPPILY MARRIED WITH VEGETABLES AND SEAFOOD TO MAKE A SALAD, WITH A LIGHT DRESSING FRAGRANT WITH GINGER AND SESAME OIL.

Lebanese (short) cucumbers	2
dried wakame seaweed pieces	1 tablespoon
dried somen noodles	100 g (3¹/2 oz)
cooked king prawns (shrimp)	12, peeled, deveined and cut in half lengthways
spring onions (scallions)	3, thinly sliced on the diagonal
shichimi togarashi (seven-spice mix)	to serve, optional

dressing

dashi granules	¹/2 teaspoon
Japanese rice vinegar	125 ml (4 fl oz/¹/2 cup)
mirin	60 ml (2 fl oz/¹/4 cup)
shoyu (Japanese soy sauce)	1 teaspoon
fresh ginger	2 teaspoons very finely grated
sugar	pinch
sesame oil	¹/2 teaspoon

Cut the cucumbers in half lengthways, scoop out the seeds with a teaspoon, then slice the flesh very thinly on a slight diagonal. Put the cucumber in a colander, sprinkle with salt and set aside for 10 minutes. Rinse, drain well and gently squeeze out as much water as you can. Chill in the refrigerator until needed.

Meanwhile, soak the wakame in cold water for 5 minutes, or until rehydrated and glossy but not mushy. Drain well and chill.

To make the dressing, mix the dashi granules with 1 tablespoon hot water until dissolved. Add the rice vinegar, mirin, shoyu, ginger, sugar and sesame oil and stir to combine. Chill.

Bring a large saucepan of water to the boil, then reduce to a simmer. Add the noodles and cook for 2 minutes, or until tender. Quickly drain and rinse under cold running water until the noodles are completely cool.

Combine the cucumber, wakame, noodles, prawns and half the spring onion in a large bowl. Pour over the dressing and toss well. Serve immediately, garnished with the remaining spring onion and, if you like, sprinkle with shichimi togarashi.

Cut the cooked king prawns in half lengthways

Scoop out the seeds from the cucumber halves

Thinly slice the cucumber, cutting on a slight diagonal

perfect edamame

Edamame, or fresh soya beans in their pods, have long been a favourite vegetable in Asia, their use recorded as far back as 2000 years ago. Traditionally, the Japanese diet included little meat, making the protein-rich soya bean a nutritious and versatile ingredient. The green soya bean pods are picked while still young and tender, and nestled within each pod are the soya beans, ranging in number from two to four. Cooking them lightly separates the bean from the pod — squeeze them at one end and the little beans will pop out the other. Today edamame are often eaten as a snack, sometimes chilled and served with a beer. The beans are also used in salads, stir-fries and soups. Edamame are available fresh when in season, and are also sold frozen.

To prepare the edamame, first rub 500 g (1 lb 2 oz) fresh soya beans in pods with salt between your hands to rub off the fine hairy fibres. Rinse the pods. If you are using frozen soya beans, this step is not necessary. Pour 1 litre (35 fl oz/4 cups) dashi I (see recipe on page 24) and 250 ml (9 fl oz/1 cup) water, or 1.25 litres (44 fl oz/5 cups) water only into a saucepan and bring to the boil over high heat. Add the soya beans and cook for 6–8 minutes if using fresh or 3–4 minutes if using frozen, or until the beans are tender but still bright green. Drain. You can serve these either warm, at room temperature or chilled. Sprinkle with about 3 teaspoons salt. To eat, simply suck the beans out of the pods and throw the pods away. Supply a bowl to collect the empty pods.

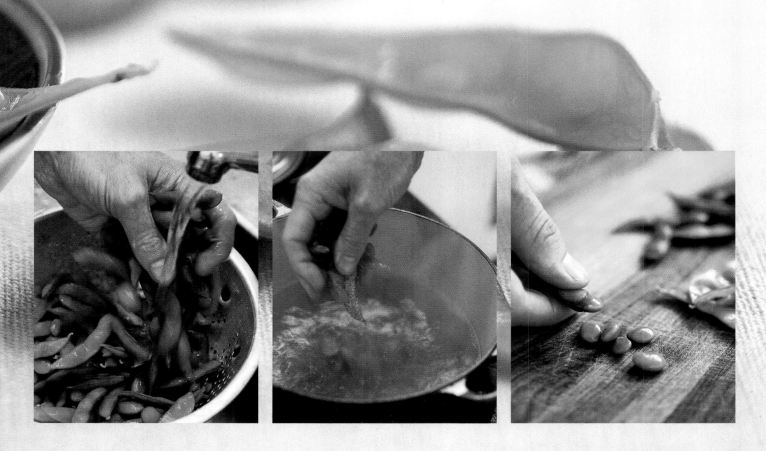

japanese coleslaw . . . . serves 6–8

THIS RECIPE, CALLING FOR CHINESE CABBAGE AND DRESSED WITH A JAPANESE-STYLE TANGY DRESSING, CREATES A COLESLAW WITH A DELIGHTFUL DIFFERENCE. THE GARNISH OF TOASTED BLACK SESAME SEEDS IS AN ARTFUL ACCENT AGAINST THE CREAMY COLOURS OF THE VEGETABLES.

Chinese cabbage	200 g (7 oz)
carrot	1, peeled
daikon	150 g (5 1/2 oz), peeled
spring onions (scallions)	2, thinly sliced on the diagonal
black sesame seeds	2 teaspoons, toasted

dressing

Japanese mayonnaise	125 g (4 1/2 oz/1/2 cup)
Japanese rice vinegar	1 1/2 tablespoons
sake	1 tablespoon
Japanese mustard or wasabi paste	1/4 teaspoon
sesame oil	1/2 teaspoon
shoyu (Japanese soy sauce)	2 teaspoons
caster (superfine) sugar	1 teaspoon
ground white pepper	to season

Finely shred the cabbage and put it in a large bowl. Cut the carrot and daikon into 5 cm (2 in) lengths, then julienne the lengths using a Japanese mandolin with the coarse-tooth blade, or coarsely grate. Place the daikon in a colander, sprinkle with salt and set aside for 15 minutes. Gently squeeze out any excess moisture with your hands.

To make the dressing, put all the ingredients in a bowl and mix until smooth. Season to taste with salt and white pepper.

Add the carrot, daikon and spring onion to the cabbage along with the sesame seeds and the dressing. Toss well, then serve.

The Japanese first tasted mayonnaise in the 19th century, after their country was forced out of its long seclusion. This French creation began to be daringly produced in Japan in 1925, and that same original brand, Kewpie, dominates the huge mayonnaise market today. It's a surprising success for a product so seemingly un-Japanese. Equally surprising are some of its uses: mixed into *onigiri* (rice ball) fillings and squirted atop *okonomiyaki* (a type of pancake) and pizza. The past decade has seen the rise of so-called *mayoraa* — mayonnaise users so enthusiastic that they even top off their bowls of rice with it, and carry with them handy packets to flavour their food when away from home.

spinach with
sesame dressing

SPINACH IS AN EXTREMELY POPULAR VEGETABLE, WHICH JAPANESE SOMETIMES JOKINGLY REFER TO AS *POPAI*, FOR THAT MUSCULAR SPINACH-LOVER OF CARTOON FAME. HERE SNUG LITTLE MOUNDS OF SPINACH, EASY TO EAT WITH FINGERS OR CHOPSTICKS, ARE TOPPED WITH A DELECTABLE SESAME PASTE.

English spinach	200 g (7 oz), stems trimmed
shoyu (Japanese soy sauce)	for sprinkling

dressing

white or black sesame seeds	50 g (1¾ oz/⅓ cup)
caster (superfine) sugar	1½ teaspoons
sake	1 tablespoon
dashi II	1½ tablespoons (see recipe on page 24)
tamari	2 teaspoons

Rinse the spinach thoroughly to remove any grit. Bring a saucepan of salted water to the boil, add the spinach and cook for 1 minute. Drain and plunge into iced water to stop the cooking process, then drain well again. Wrap in a bamboo sushi mat or tea towel (dish towel) and squeeze out any excess water. Sprinkle lightly with a little shoyu, allow to cool, then cut into 3 cm (1¼ in) lengths and place on a serving platter.

To make the dressing, dry-fry the sesame seeds over medium heat, stirring regularly, for about 5 minutes, or until lightly toasted and aromatic. Immediately scoop into a mortar or a *suribachi* (Japanese ribbed mortar), reserving 1 teaspoon of whole seeds for garnish, and grind with the pestle until very finely crushed. Gradually incorporate the sugar, sake, dashi and tamari until it forms a smooth paste. Spoon some of the sesame paste on top of each spinach bundle. Sprinkle with the reserved toasted sesame seeds and serve.

Briefly plunge the cooked spinach into iced water, then drain well

Wrap the spinach in a sushi mat and squeeze out any water

When cool, cut the spinach into short lengths

miso tofu sticks with cucumber and wakame salad ....serves 4

THESE DENSE AND DELICIOUS GRILLED (BROILED) TOFU STICKS, WITH THEIR GOLDEN GLAZE OF MISO AND EGG YOLK, MAKE AN UNCOMMON TOPPING FOR THIS VEGETARIAN SALAD. THE CUCUMBERS AND BEAN SPROUTS OFFER A CRISPY FRESHNESS, AND THE WAKAME GIVES A HINT OF THE SEA.

Lebanese (short) cucumbers	3, thinly sliced
dried wakame seaweed pieces	20 g (3/4 oz/1/2 cup)
silken firm tofu	500 g (1 lb 2 oz), well drained
white miso paste	3 tablespoons
mirin	1 tablespoon
sugar	1 tablespoon
rice vinegar	1 tablespoon
egg yolk	1
bean sprouts	100 g (3 1/2 oz), blanched
sesame seeds	2 tablespoons, toasted

dressing

rice vinegar	60 ml (2 fl oz/1/4 cup)
shoyu (Japanese soy sauce)	1/4 teaspoon
sugar	1 1/2 tablespoons
mirin	1 tablespoon

Sprinkle the cucumber generously with salt and set aside for 20 minutes, or until very soft, then rinse and drain. Squeeze out any excess water. Refrigerate until needed. Soak the wakame in cold water for 5 minutes, or until rehydrated and glossy but not mushy. Drain well, then refrigerate until needed.

Place the tofu in a colander, put two plates on top of the tofu and leave for about 30 minutes to extract any excess moisture. Put the miso, mirin, sugar, rice vinegar and 2 tablespoons water in a saucepan and stir over low heat for 1 minute, or until the sugar dissolves. Remove from the heat, add the egg yolk and whisk until glossy. Cool slightly.

Cut the tofu into thick sticks and put on a non-stick baking tray. Brush the miso mixture over the tofu and cook under a hot grill (broiler) for 6 minutes each side, or until the tofu is light golden.

To make the dressing, put all the ingredients and 1/2 teaspoon salt in a bowl and whisk together well.

To assemble, place the cucumber in the centre of a plate, top with the bean sprouts and wakame, drizzle with the dressing, then top with tofu and serve sprinkled with sesame seeds.

Sprinkle the cucumber with salt, then set aside

To rehydrate the wakame, soak it in cold water

Add the egg yolk to the miso mixture and whisk until glossy

eggplant with dashi............................serves 6–8

THE EGGPLANT (AUBERGINE), *NASU*, IS ONE OF THE FAVOURITE SUMMER VEGETABLES IN JAPANESE CUISINE, AND ALSO, INCIDENTALLY, A POPULAR DECORATIVE MOTIF ON TABLEWARE. ITS TENDER TEXTURE AND MILDNESS ARE WELL SUITED TO THE FLAVOURED DASHI SEASONING IN THIS DISH.

baby or slender eggplants (aubergines)	6
oil	for brushing
dashi II	60 ml (2 fl oz/¼ cup) (see recipe on page 24)
shoyu (Japanese soy sauce)	1½ tablespoons
mirin	1 teaspoon
fresh ginger	½ teaspoon grated, and its juice
caster (superfine) sugar	pinch
fine katsuobushi (bonito flakes)	to garnish

Preheat a grill (broiler) to high. Brush the eggplants with oil, then prick a few times with a skewer. Put the eggplants under the grill and cook for 12–15 minutes, turning regularly, until the skin is slightly blackened and wrinkled and the flesh feels soft to the touch. Immediately plunge into iced water until cool enough to handle, then peel, discarding the skin. Cut the flesh into 5 cm (2 in) lengths. Arrange in a bundle in a serving dish.

Combine the dashi, shoyu, mirin, ginger and juice, and sugar and pour over the eggplant. Sprinkle the katsuobushi over the top of the eggplants just before serving.

Katsuobushi, or bonito flakes, is a unique flavouring ingredient essential to everyday cooking. Fillets of bonito fish, called *katsuo*, are steamed, smoked, mould-cured and dried hard as wood. Traditionally, a special tool called a *katsuobushi-bako* was used to plane off the shavings needed, but today most cooks find packets of pre-shaved flakes (sold in large and fine grades) to be more convenient. These smoky fish flakes are frequently the base for dashi stock, and through dashi, they lend their flavour to other dishes too. Pink in colour, and seemingly lighter-than-air, the shavings make a tasty and visually appealing garnish for cold soba noodles, rice, tofu and vegetable dishes.

sweet simmered pumpkin

NUGGETS OF GOLDEN-ORANGE PUMPKIN (WINTER SQUASH) ARE INFUSED WITH THE WONDERFUL FLAVOURS OF THEIR SIMMERING, SWEET LIQUID. MAKE THIS VEGETABLE EXTRA NUTRITIOUS AND MORE ATTRACTIVE BY LEAVING SOME OF THE DARK GREEN SKIN ON.

jap, kent or butternut pumpkin (winter squash)	700 g (1 lb 9 oz), unpeeled
dashi II	185 ml (6 fl oz/¾ cup) (see recipe on page 24)
mirin	2 tablespoons
shoyu (Japanese soy sauce)	1½ tablespoons
caster (superfine) sugar	3 teaspoons
sesame seeds	toasted, to garnish

Cut the pumpkin into rough 4 cm (1½ in) cubes. Peel just around the edges of the skin on each piece, then run a sharp knife or a vegetable peeler along the sharp edges so the cube shape is softened and slightly rounded.

Put the pumpkin into a saucepan and cover with cold water. Bring to the boil over high heat and cook for about 5 minutes, or until it just begins to become tender. Drain well.

Combine the dashi, mirin, shoyu, sugar and ½ teaspoon salt in a clean saucepan over high heat, stirring until the sugar has dissolved. Add the pumpkin, skin side down, and bring the liquid to the boil. Reduce to a simmer, then continue cooking for about 15 minutes, or until the liquid has almost all been absorbed by the pumpkin. Do not stir but carefully turn once halfway through the cooking time.

Carefully pile the pumpkin into a serving bowl, drizzle with any remaining sauce and sprinkle with toasted sesame seeds.

Use a sharp knife to soften the edges of the pumpkin cubes

Put the pumpkin, skin side down, into the dashi mixture

Cook for 15 minutes, turning the pumpkin over halfway through

shiitake simmered in soy .... serves 4–6

DRIED SHIITAKE ARE PRIZED IN CERTAIN RECIPES FOR THEIR MORE PRONOUNCED NATURAL TASTE AND DENSER TEXTURE THAN THEIR FRESH COUNTERPART. IT IS PRECISELY THESE QUALITIES THAT MAKE IT THE MUSHROOM OF CHOICE FOR THIS SLOW-SIMMERED AND INTENSELY FLAVOURFUL SIDE DISH.

dried shiitake mushrooms	8 large
dashi II or konbu dashi II	375 ml (13 fl oz/1 1/2 cups) (see recipes on page 24)
mirin	2 tablespoons
sake	2 tablespoons
shoyu (Japanese soy sauce)	2 tablespoons
dark brown sugar	1 tablespoon

Soak the shiitake in hot water for 30 minutes, then drain well. Discard the stems.

Combine the dashi, mirin, sake, shoyu and sugar in a small saucepan. Put the pan over high heat and stir until the sugar has dissolved. Bring to the boil. Add the shiitake, return to the boil, then reduce to a simmer and cook for 1 hour, or until the liquid has almost evaporated.

Serve the shiitake in a small bowl either warm or at room temperature as a condiment, part of a multicourse meal or served over rice as a snack. Simmered shiitake can also be thinly sliced to use in sushi (see recipes on pages 100 and 110) or savoury Japanese custard.

Since ancient times, wild shiitake were gathered from Japanese forests where they thrive on fallen and decaying trees, often a variety of oak called *shii*, for which they were named. Today these delicious mushrooms are big business for cultivators. Dark brown in colour, with pale undersides and stems, shiitake exude a woodsy aroma and deep flavour. Fresh and dried each have their own role in recipes and are not considered interchangeable. After soaking the dried mushrooms, their soaking water can be used in a vegetarian stock or to add flavour to other dishes. Shiitake are said to have impressive nutritional and medicinal benefits.

sushi

Of all Japanese foods, sushi is probably the best known outside of its homeland. The introduction to sushi can be a gustatory awakening. This combination of lightly vinegared and seasoned rice, with a touch of wasabi and any of dozens of possible toppings, raw fish primary among them, has delighted myriad adventurous diners around the world in recent years.

The origins of sushi lie in the ancient Asian custom of preserving raw fish in fermenting rice, and such *nare-zushi* can still be eaten in a few remote villages, although to outsiders its strong taste is usually unappealing. Sushi, as we know it today, is a product of late 17th century Edo (old Tokyo). Right up to the 1950s it was not sold in shops, but rather by roving street peddlers who carried their goods in boxes, carefully balanced on poles across their shoulders.

In a good *sushi-ya*, sushi bar, the chef has probably devoted 10 years of his life to apprenticeship. The first 4 years, he (for it is almost always a man) only observed the master and performed basic and peripheral chores, while never being permitted to actually wield a knife on fish. Watching the experienced chef is a great show, as every precise cut and gesture has been perfected by endless repetition.

Making good *nigiri-zushi*, hand-moulded sushi, is rather challenging, so Japanese housewives sometimes hesitate to attempt it themselves unless they have first taken a class to learn some techniques. Other simpler versions, however, are very popular among home cooks. With a few simple practice rolls using the bamboo *makisu* mat, a novice can quickly learn to turn out snug and attractive *maki-zushi*. One cannot go wrong with *chirashi-zushi*, which features a variety of sushi toppings artfully scattered atop a platter or tray of rice. Another favourite kind of home-made sushi is *temaki-zushi*, which is hand-rolled by the diners into a cone of nori from an assortment of ingredients set out on the table. This hands-on experience makes for a particularly festive and convivial meal.

Whether made in a sushi bar or at home, sushi involves certain absolutes. Above all, the seafood must be extremely fresh, and purchased from a dealer who understands that it will likely be eaten raw. Chefs also emphasize the importance of a good sharp knife, if possible one that has been specifically made for slicing fish for sushi. And, a light touch is called for — the ingredients should be handled as little as possible.

inari sushi . . . . makes 20 pieces

THESE DELECTABLE LITTLE BUNDLES OF VINEGARED RICE IN POCKETS OF DEEP-FRIED TOFU CAN SERVE AS A STARTER, SNACK OR EVEN LUNCH BOX FARE. FRESH GREEN CHIVE TIES ADD A DECORATIVE TOUCH AND THE CLUSTER OF PINK PICKLED GINGER PROVIDES COLOUR AND FLAVOUR CONTRASTS.

inari abura-age (prepared deep-fried tofu sheets)	20 pieces
sushi rice	1 quantity (see recipe on page 104)
chives	20, optional
shoyu (Japanese soy sauce)	to serve
wasabi paste	to serve, optional
pickled ginger	to serve, optional

Put the prepared abura-age in a colander and drain off any excess liquid. Carefully insert a finger into the slit side of each sheet and gently prise the pocket open, trying not to split them.

Fill each pocket with 2 tablespoons of the prepared sushi rice, then fold over the open ends to enclose the rice as much as possible. You can dress these up by tying a chive around the middle and securing with a knot at the top — this also helps hold the open ends together to prevent the rice from falling out. Put the sushi rice pockets, seam side down, on a platter.

Serve with a small bowl of shoyu for dipping into and, if desired, a little wasabi paste on the side to mix into the sauce and some pickled ginger as a palate refresher.

Abura-age is thinly sliced, deep-fried tofu. Often slivered and used as an ingredient in soups and soba, it is also sometimes sliced in half (to reveal the air pocket that formed in the middle during frying) and stuffed. Simmered in a sweetened soy sauce broth and filled with seasoned sushi rice, these pockets of *abura-age* become *Inari-zushi*. With pickled ginger served on the side, they are an immensely popular food for snacks, lunches and picnics. And why *Inari*? Well, Inari-san is the deity of grains and harvest. Inari's messenger is the fox who, it is said, has a great liking for *abura-age*, so much so that it is often left as an offering at Inari shrines.

california rolls

ROLLED SUSHI IS EASY TO MAKE, SO EVEN THE NOVICE CAN SUCCEED ON THE FIRST TRY. CALIFORNIA ROLLS, BURSTING WITH A VARIETY OF LAVISH FILLINGS, WERE INSPIRED BY AMERICAN FREE-PLAY WITH SUSHI CLASSICS, AND THEY HAVE RECENTLY ALSO BECOME STYLISH IN JAPAN.

egg	1 large
sake	1 teaspoon
sugar	pinch
oil	1 teaspoon
nori sheets	2, toasted, 20 x 18 cm (8 x 7 in)
sushi rice	1/2 quantity (see recipe on page 104)
crabsticks	2, 40 g (1 1/2 oz) each, cut into strips
pickled daikon	25 g (1 oz/1/4 cup), cut into julienne strips
carrot	4 cm (1 1/2 in) piece, (25 g/1 oz), cut into julienne strips
cucumber	4 cm (1 1/2 in) piece, (25 g/1 oz), cut into julienne strips
shoyu (Japanese soy sauce)	to serve
wasabi paste	to serve
pickled ginger	to serve

To make an omelette, gently combine the egg, sake, a pinch of sugar and a pinch of salt. Heat the oil in a small frying pan. Pour in the egg mixture and cook until firm around the edges but still slightly soft in the middle. Roll up the omelette, then tip it out of the pan. Cool, then slice into strips.

Put a nori sheet on a sushi mat, shiny side down. Add half of the prepared sushi rice, leaving a 4 cm (1 1/2 in) gap at the edge furthest away from you. Lay half of the fillings on the rice in the following order: omelette strips, crabstick, daikon, carrot and cucumber. Holding the filling in place with your fingertips and starting with the end nearest to you, roll the sushi away from you, tightly rolling the mat and the nori. When the roll is finished, press the mat down to form a neat, firm roll. Unroll the mat and put the roll, seam side down, on a cutting board. Repeat this process with the remaining ingredients to make a second roll.

Using a sharp knife, trim the ends and cut each roll into six slices. After cutting each slice, rinse the knife under cold running water to prevent sticking. Serve with shoyu, wasabi and pickled ginger.

Starting with the end nearest to you, roll up the sushi in the mat

Cut each roll into six slices, rinsing the knife after each slice

hand-moulded sushi..makes 20

TUNA, SALMON AND PRAWNS (SHRIMP) ARE AMONG THE MOST POPULAR OF ALL THE VARIETIES OF TOPPINGS FOR SUSHI. IN CONTRAST TO ROLLED STYLES, HERE THE WASABI IS PLACED BETWEEN THE RICE AND TOPPING, AND THE SHAPING OF THE RICE MOUNDS IS DONE BY HAND.

cooked prawns (shrimp)	10
Japanese rice vinegar	1 tablespoon
sushi rice	1/2 quantity
	(see recipe on page 104)
sashimi-grade tuna or salmon	10 slices
wasabi paste	for spreading, plus extra to serve
shoyu (Japanese soy sauce)	to serve
pickled ginger	to serve

Peel the prawns, leaving the tails intact if desired, then use a small knife to slit the prawns along their bellies, ensuring you don't cut through to the other side. Turn the prawn over and carefully remove the intestinal tract.

Fill a bowl with warm water and mix in the rice vinegar. Dampen your hands with the vinegared water to prevent the sushi rice sticking to your hands. Form a slightly heaped tablespoon of rice into a rounded rectangle about 5 x 2 cm (2 x 3/4 in), wetting your hands as needed. Put on a tray lined with plastic wrap, then cover with a damp tea towel (dish towel). Repeat with the remaining rice — you should get about 20 mounds.

Put a slice of tuna or salmon sashimi in the palm of your left hand, then use a finger on your right hand to smear a little wasabi over the top. Put a piece of the moulded rice along the fish, gently cup your left palm to make a slight curve, then using the middle and index fingers of your right hand, press the rice firmly onto the fish, keeping the shape as neat and compact as possible. Turn the fish over so it is facing upwards, then neaten up the shape, keeping your left hand flat. Place, rice side down, on a plate and cover with plastic wrap while you repeat with the rest of the fish. Repeat the same process with the prawns, which should have the belly side against the rice.

Serve with a small bowl of shoyu for dipping into and, if desired, a little extra wasabi on the side to mix into the sauce and some pickled ginger as a palate refresher. Eat with your fingers and dip the fish side, not the rice side, into the dipping sauce.

Make a small cut along the belly of the prawn

Press the fish onto the rice, then turn it over and neaten the shape

three ways with condiments

JAPANESE CUISINE HAS A WHOLE WORLD OF FASCINATING CONDIMENTS TO EXPLORE. WITH A WIDE VARIETY TO CHOOSE FROM, PICKLES ACCOMPANY EVERY TRADITIONAL MEAL, EVEN BREAKFAST. PICKLED GINGER IS ESSENTIAL TO SUSHI, AND PICKLED PLUMS A DELIGHT WITH RICE. DRIED BONITO FLAKES TOP TOFU, AND SHICHIMI TOGARASHI PERKS UP YAKITORI, AS WELL AS HOT SOBA OR UDON. RICE MAY BE SPRINKLED OR TOSSED WITH A SEASONING THAT CAN INCLUDE INGREDIENTS SUCH AS NORI FLAKES, SESAME SEEDS OR TINY DRIED FISH.

pickled ginger

Put 250 g (9 oz) thinly sliced peeled fresh ginger in a heatproof bowl. Combine 250 ml (9 fl oz/1 cup) Japanese rice vinegar and 2 tablespoons sugar in a small saucepan. Add 125 ml (4 fl oz/½ cup) water and bring to the boil, stirring to dissolve the sugar. Pour over the ginger and allow to cool. Cover and refrigerate for at least 2 days before eating. Pickled ginger keeps well in the refrigerator for several weeks. Makes 250 g (9 oz).

rice seasoning

Heat a non-stick frying pan over high heat and dry-fry 2 tablespoons white sesame seeds and 2 teaspoons black sesame seeds until they begin to pop and the white seeds turn golden brown. Place in a bowl and allow to cool. Stir in 1 teaspoon salt, ½ teaspoon ichimi (ground chilli mixture), 2 tablespoons nori flakes and 1 tablespoon shiso furikake (rice seasoning). Sprinkle over cooked rice, to taste. Makes about 125 g (4½ oz/½ cup).

shichimi togarashi

Grind 2 teaspoons sancho or sichuan peppercorns and 1 teaspoon white sesame seeds using a mortar and pestle or a spice grinder. Combine with 1 teaspoon black sesame seeds, 2 teaspoons crushed dried tangerine peel, 1 teaspoon finely chopped nori, 1 teaspoon chilli powder and 1 teaspoon poppy seeds. Store in an airtight container for up to 1 month. Makes 2 tablespoons.

pickled ginger

layered sushi . . . . makes 36

THESE APPEALING LAYERED SQUARES ARE A NOVEL AND EASY WAY TO SERVE SUSHI, WHILE THE DOLLOP OF SPICY MAYONNAISE TOPPING ADDS A SPECIAL TOUCH. THEY WOULD BE AS WELCOME AS A STARTER COURSE AT DINNER AS THEY WOULD BE ON A PARTY BUFFET TABLE.

Japanese mayonnaise	60 g (2¼ oz/¼ cup)
wasabi paste	1 teaspoon
nori sheets	3, toasted
sushi rice	½ quantity
	(see recipe on page 104)
smoked salmon	200 g (7 oz)
pickled ginger	40 g (1½ oz/¼ cup)
black sesame seeds	to garnish

Combine the mayonnaise and wasabi in a small bowl. Lay a sheet of nori, shiny side up, on top of a piece of baking paper on a dry tray. Entirely cover the nori with half of the prepared sushi rice. Spread with a little of the wasabi mayonnaise, then top with a layer of smoked salmon and some slices of pickled ginger. Place another sheet of nori on top and flatten lightly with a rolling pin. Repeat the layering again, to form two layers, finishing with a sheet of nori, and again flattening with the rolling pin. Reserve the remaining wasabi mayonnaise.

Cover and refrigerate for at least 1 hour, then, using a very sharp knife dipped in water, trim any filling protruding from the edges and slice the sushi into 2 cm (¾ in) squares. Top with some of the reserved wasabi mayonnaise, sprinkle with black sesame seeds and serve with the remaining pickled ginger.

Cover the rice with a layer of smoked salmon

Cover with a sheet of nori and gently flatten with a rolling pin

hand-rolled sushi . . . . makes 18

HAND-ROLLED SUSHI IS AN ENTERTAINING CHOICE FOR A CASUAL MEAL AMONG FAMILY OR FRIENDS, WITH ACTIVE PARTICIPATION CONDUCIVE TO FUN AND CONVERSATION. THE FILLINGS LISTED HERE ARE ONLY SUGGESTIONS — FEEL FREE TO TRY YOUR OWN COMBINATION OF INGREDIENTS.

sushi rice	1/2 quantity (see recipe on page 104)
nori sheets	9, toasted
shoyu (Japanese soy sauce)	to serve
wasabi paste	to serve
pickled ginger	to serve
Japanese rice vinegar	1 tablespoon

fillings

crabmeat	175 g (6 oz) tinned, drained
Japanese mayonnaise	2 tablespoons
Lebanese (short) cucumber	1, cut in half, then into long thin strips
avocado	1, thinly sliced
smoked salmon	100 g (3 1/2 oz), cut into strips

Put the prepared sushi rice into a serving dish. Using scissors or a very sharp knife, cut each nori sheet in half.

For the fillings, combine the crabmeat with the mayonnaise, then heap it neatly on a platter. Arrange the other fillings on the same platter. Put the rice, nori, fillings, shoyu, wasabi and pickled ginger in the centre of the dining table for each person to make their own sushi.

Add a little rice vinegar to bowls of warm water and put these on the table — by dampening your hands in the vinegared water you will prevent the rice from sticking to your hands. To roll the sushi, put the rectangle of nori in your left palm. Take a heaped tablespoon of rice and form it into a rough oblong, then put it not quite in the centre, but just slightly towards the left edge of the nori. Add one or several of the fillings along the length of the rice, being careful not to add too much or the rolls will split. Roll up into a cone, rolling from left to right, and eat immediately.

Wasabi grows wild in and along clear mountain streams, and is also cultivated in flooded mountain fields. This freshly grated knobbly root is used to add aroma and fire to dipping sauces, dressings, raw seafood and tofu. A small grater with a sharkskin surface is the best and traditional tool for this task, although metal graters are more commonly used. It is often difficult to find fresh wasabi outside of Japan, and even in Japan only some of the better supermarkets stock it. Fresh wasabi is usually replaced in recipes by commercial wasabi paste or Western horseradish paste with added green colouring, sold in convenient and economical tubes.

rolled sushi . . . . makes 4 thick rolls or 24 thick pieces

TOASTED NORI SEAWEED IS USED TO WRAP THESE SIMPLE VEGETARIAN SUSHI ROLLS, WHICH ARE FILLED WITH VARIOUS TEXTURES AND TASTES — FROM CHEWY GOURD TO MOIST TOFU AND SOY-FLAVOURED MUSHROOMS. ROLLED SUSHI IS EASY TO MAKE, AS THE TECHNIQUE FOR USING THE BAMBOO *MAKISU* IS QUICKLY MASTERED.

Japanese rice vinegar	1 tablespoon
nori sheets	4, toasted
sushi rice	1 quantity
	(see recipe on page 104)
wasabi paste	for spreading, plus extra to serve
shoyu (Japanese soy sauce)	to serve
pickled ginger	to serve

filling

prepared kanpyo (gourd strip)	30 g (1 oz) (see note and
	photograph, page 110)
firm tofu	100 g (3$^{1}/_2$ oz), cut into long strips
	about 1 cm ($^{1}/_2$ in) thick and wide
simmered shiitake mushrooms	85 g (3 oz), thinly sliced
	(see recipe on page 82)
pickled daikon	100 g (3$^{1}/_2$ oz), cut into 1 cm
	($^{1}/_2$ in) thick strips

Fill a bowl with warm water and mix in the rice vinegar. Lay a nori sheet, shiny side down, on a bamboo mat with the short end of the mat towards you. Dampen your hands with the vinegared water to prevent the rice sticking to your hands. Starting at the edge nearest to you and stopping about 4 cm (1$^{1}/_2$ in) from the edge furthest from you, spread about 280 g (10 oz/1$^{1}/_2$ cups) prepared sushi rice over the nori, pressing the rice down with your fingers — the rice should be about 1 cm ($^{1}/_2$ in) thick. Wet your hands as needed.

About 8 cm (3$^{1}/_4$ in) in from the end closest to you, use your finger to smear a little wasabi paste along the width of the roll. Take one type of filling at a time and lay it along the wasabi paste so that you have a long strip across the rice. Repeat with the other ingredients, placing each one snugly on top of and next to the other, then trim the edges.

Holding the filling in place with the tips of your fingers, lift the closest end of the bamboo mat with your thumbs and, holding everything taut, roll the sushi away from you, making sure you do not tuck the edge of the mat under the roll. When the roll is finished, press the mat down over the top to form a neat, firm roll. Unroll the mat and put the sushi roll, seam side down, on a cutting board. Repeat with the remaining ingredients to make four sushi rolls.

Using a very sharp, large knife, trim the ends of each roll. Dip the knife into water after each slice to prevent the rice from sticking to it and cut each roll into six to eight pieces. Arrange the pieces, cut side up, on a platter.

Serve with a small bowl of shoyu for dipping into and, if desired, extra wasabi to mix into the sauce and some pickled ginger as a palate refresher.

Lay the fillings in a strip across the rice

Roll up the sushi, being careful not to tuck the mat under the roll

pressed sushi .... makes 16 pieces

FRESH SWEET PRAWNS (SHRIMP) MAKE A LUXURIOUS AND APPEALING TOPPING FOR THIS EASY-TO-MAKE SUSHI. LAYERED BETWEEN DARK GREEN NORI AND RICE, THE CENTRE HIDES JEWEL-LIKE ORANGE FISH ROE, WHICH BURST WITH THE SALTY FLAVOUR OF THE SEA WITH EVERY BITE. ·

cooked king prawns (shrimp)	16
Japanese rice vinegar	2 tablespoons, plus 1 tablespoon extra
caster (superfine) sugar	1 teaspoon
wasabi paste	optional
sushi rice	1 quantity (see recipe on page 104)
flying fish roe or salmon roe	125 g (4½ oz)
nori sheets	4, toasted

Line a 26 x 16 cm (10½ x 6¼ in) baking tin, about 4 cm (1½ in) deep, with two long pieces of plastic wrap so that it overhangs on all sides. You will also need another slightly smaller tin or dish.

Peel the prawns, then use a small knife to slit them along their bellies, ensuring you don't cut through to the other side. Carefully remove the intestinal tract. Mix the vinegar with the sugar and a pinch of salt, stirring until the sugar has dissolved, then add the prawns and mix. Set aside for 15 minutes. Drain well, then neatly and snugly arrange the prawns in a single layer, belly side up, in the baking tin. Flatten the prawns with your hands, then smear a little wasabi over the cut side of each prawn, if you are using it.

Fill a bowl with warm water and mix in the extra vinegar. Dampen your hands with the water to prevent the rice sticking to your hands. Carefully spread half the prepared sushi rice over the prawns, without moving the prawns, then press down firmly. Smooth the rice over so that it forms an even layer, wetting your hands as needed.

Spead the roe over the rice in a thin even layer using the back of a spoon, then press down gently. Trim two of the nori sheets to fit the tin and cover the rice in a single layer. Press down to adhere. Add the remaining rice, pressing and smoothing as you did earlier, then trim the remaining two nori sheets to cover the rice and press down again to adhere.

Fold the plastic wrap over the sides to enclose the rice. Put the smaller tin on top of the plastic and fill with cold water to weigh down the sushi. Leave for 30 minutes, then remove the tin. Unfold the plastic wrap and invert the sushi onto a platter. Remove the plastic carefully so the prawns stay in place. Use a knife to cut into 16 rectangles.

Spread the rice over the layer of prawns and press down firmly

Spread the fish roe over the rice using the back of a spoon

perfect sushi rice

Sushi is made using a type of short-grain rice, sometimes called sticky rice, and is prepared with sweetened vinegar. Once cooked, the rice grains stick together, making it ideal for sushi or for eating with chopsticks. Sushi takes on many forms, the most familiar being *nigiri-zushi*, a pillow of rice topped with raw fish or seafood, and *maki-zushi*, a sheet of nori topped with rice and various fillings and then rolled into a cylinder.

To prepare sushi rice, rinse 550 g (1 lb 4 oz/2½ cups) Japanese short-grain white rice several times in cold water or until the water runs clear, then drain in a colander for 1 hour. Put the rice in a saucepan with 750 ml (26 fl oz/3 cups) cold water and, if you like, add a 4 cm (1½ in) piece of konbu (kelp), wiped with a damp cloth, and 2 tablespoons sake. Bring to the boil, then remove the konbu. Cover with a tight-fitting lid, reduce the heat to low and simmer for 15 minutes. Turn off the heat but leave the pan on the hotplate. Working quickly, remove the lid and place a clean tea towel (dish towel) across the top (to absorb excess moisture), then put the lid on for a further 15 minutes. Alternatively, cook the rice in a rice cooker, following the manufacturer's instructions.

Transfer the cooked rice into a wide, shallow non-metallic container and spread it out. Combine 80 ml (2½ fl oz/⅓ cup) Japanese rice vinegar, 1½ tablespoons caster (superfine) sugar and ½ teaspoon salt, stirring until the sugar has dissolved, then sprinkle the vinegar mixture over the warm rice. Using quick, short strokes, mix the rice and liquid together with a damp wooden rice paddle or thin wooden spoon or spatula, being careful not to mush the rice. Traditionally the rice is cooled with a hand-held fan while mixing the liquid into the rice. When cooled, cover with a clean, damp tea towel. For the best results, use the rice immediately and do not refrigerate it. However, if you are not making your sushi within 1–2 hours, the rice must be refrigerated or bacteria may develop. Makes 1 quantity or 1.1 kg (2 lb 7 oz/6 cups) cooked rice.

nori cones .... makes 40

NORI CONES FILLED WITH RICE AND VEGETABLES, SEASONED WITH WASABI AND AROMATIC SOUTHEAST ASIAN KECAP MANIS, MAKE A RATHER UNCOMMON, BUT DELICIOUS, SUSHI. SERVE THEM AS PART OF A SUSHI PLATTER ASSORTMENT OR AS ONE AMONG SEVERAL PARTY NIBBLES.

dried shiitake mushrooms	3
sushi rice	1 quantity
	(see recipe on page 104)
choy sum (Chinese flowering cabbage)	250 g (9 oz) shredded, blanched
pickled ginger	1 tablespoon shredded
sesame seeds	1 tablespoon, toasted
kecap manis	1 tablespoon
wasabi paste	1/2 teaspoon
mirin	2 teaspoons
shoyu (Japanese soy sauce)	1 tablespoon
nori sheets	10, toasted
sushi dipping sauce	ready-made, to serve

Soak the shiitake in hot water for 30 minutes, then drain well. Discard the stems. Squeeze dry and roughly chop.

Put the prepared sushi rice in a bowl and stir in the shiitake, choy sum, pickled ginger, sesame seeds and the combined kecap manis, wasabi, mirin and shoyu.

Lay the nori sheets, shiny side down, on the work surface and cut each one into four squares. Brush the joining edge with water and put 1 tablespoon of the mixture in the centre of the square. Roll up on the diagonal to form a cone and top up with 2 teaspoons of filling. Repeat with the remaining nori sheets and filling. Serve with the dipping sauce.

Combine the sushi rice and filling ingredients in a bowl

Roll up the nori on the diagonal to form a cone

sushi crepes

A PAPER-THIN EGG WRAP IS A DELICIOUS AND ATTRACTIVE VARIATION ON THE MORE USUAL NORI. THE CONTRAST OF ITS YELLOW WITH THE RED OF TUNA AND THE GREENS OF CUCUMBER AND AVOCADO MAKE THESE A VISUAL TREAT ON ANY SUSHI PLATTER.

eggs	4
sushi rice	¹/₂ quantity
	(see recipe on page 104)
wasabi paste	for spreading
sashimi-grade tuna	125 g (4¹/₂ oz), cut into thin strips
cucumber	1 small, peeled and cut into
	julienne strips
avocado	¹/₂, cut into julienne strips
pickled ginger	3 tablespoons, cut into thin strips
shoyu (Japanese soy sauce)	to serve

To make the crepes, gently whisk the eggs with 2 tablespoons cold water and a pinch of salt in a bowl until combined. Heat and lightly oil a small crepe pan or heavy-based frying pan and pour enough of the egg mixture into the pan to lightly cover the base. Cook over low heat for 1 minute, being careful not to allow the crepe to brown. Turn the crepe over and cook for 1 minute. Transfer to a plate and repeat with the remaining mixture to make three more crepes.

Place one egg crepe on a bamboo mat. Spread 4 tablespoons of the prepared sushi rice over the centre-third of the crepe, using a spatula or the back of a spoon. Spread a small amount of wasabi along the centre of the rice. Put some tuna, cucumber, avocado and ginger over the wasabi.

Using the sushi mat to help you, fold the crepe over to enclose the filling and roll up firmly in the mat. Trim the ends using a sharp knife and cut the roll into 2 cm (³/4 in) rounds using a sharp knife. Serve immediately with shoyu for dipping.

Note: The unfilled crepes can be made ahead and stored in an airtight container in the refrigerator.

Pour in enough of the egg to lightly cover the base of the pan

Cook over low heat, taking care that the crepe doesn't brown

Place the filling ingredients in a long strip across the rice

scattered sushi . . . . serves 4–6 as a main or 8 as a starter

SCATTERED SUSHI IS NOT ONLY EASY TO PREPARE BUT WITH ITS ABUNDANT AND COLOURFUL TOPPINGS MAKES AN IMMENSELY APPETIZING AND FESTIVE MEAL. THIS DISH IS TYPICALLY PRESENTED AT THE TABLE IN A HANDSOME WOOD OR LACQUERED BOWL.

sushi rice	1 quantity still warm (see recipe on page 104)
white, black or mixed sesame seeds	2 tablespoons, toasted
spring onions (scallions)	2, sliced
simmered shiitake mushrooms	60 g (2 1/4 oz), finely chopped (see recipe on page 82)
bamboo shoots	50 g (1 3/4 oz), finely chopped
prepared kanpyo (gourd strip)	60 g (2 1/4 oz), finely chopped
pickled ginger	2 tablespoons, finely chopped
Japanese rice vinegar	1 tablespoon
thin crepe-like omelettes	4, cut into very thin strips (see recipe on page 139)
sugar snap peas	12, trimmed, blanched
fresh or frozen peas	80 g (2 3/4 oz/1/2 cup), cooked
sashimi-grade tuna or salmon	100 g (3 1/2 oz), cut into short, thin strips
cooked king prawns (shrimp)	12, peeled and deveined
nori sheets	2, toasted, cut into thin strips

Combine the sushi rice with the sesame seeds, spring onion, shiitake, bamboo shoots, kanpyo and pickled ginger in a large bowl. Spread the mixture over the base of a large, wide shallow serving bowl or lacquerware tray with sides.

Fill a bowl with warm water and mix in the vinegar. Dampen your hands with the water to prevent the rice sticking to your hands. Smooth the rice mixture into the serving bowl, dampening your hands as needed.

Sprinkle the omelette strips evenly over the top, then arrange or scatter the peas, sashimi strips, prawns and nori strips evenly over the top. Serve immediately. Use a wooden rice paddle or spoon to serve into small bowls.

Kanpyo comes from the bottle gourd, which the Japanese call *yuugao*, commonly thought of as a vegetable but, in fact, a fruit. *Yuugao* are harvested in mid-summer and their ripe flesh is shaved into long thin strips to be dried. Although now carried out on a large commercial scale using dryers, in the past, sun drying was quite common, and *kanpyo* hanging from bamboo poles around farmhouses made a picturesque summer scene. To prepare for use, most popularly as a filling in *maki-zushi*, the dry fibrous strips are rehydrated and then simmered in a seasoned soy sauce or dashi broth. Used like ribbons, they make edible and visually pleasing ties for certain recipes.

mains

The early adoption of Buddhism and its vegetarian laws meant that for over a thousand years meat hardly ever appeared on Japanese tables. Only when the prohibition was lifted by Emperor Meiji in the late 19th century, when Western influences began to trickle into the land, did people begin to add meat, little by little, into their diets.

Today meat is extremely well liked, particularly among the younger generations. However, it is still eaten in much smaller quantities than in the West due to tradition, as well as its comparatively high cost. Surrounded as Japan is by water, however, it is only natural that a substantial part of the diet would be made up of the huge variety of available fresh seafood. These protein sources are the centrepiece of many main dishes, prepared in diverse ways — pan-fried, deep-fried, grilled (broiled) or cooked in broth.

Meat appears far more often sliced paper thin, and included in small quantities with a variety of other ingredients, than served up as steak. Accompanied with a platter of assorted cut vegetables, beef is part of several popular one-dish meals prepared at the table by the diners themselves. *Teppanyaki*, small pieces of meat and vegetables seared on a hot iron plate, and *shabu-shabu*, named for the sound of hot broth bubbling around its meat and vegetable ingredients as diners place them in the common iron pot, provide pleasurable and convivial winter meals among family and friends.

Other vegetable-rich hotpots, called *nabemono*, also make great cold-weather dishes. Cooked in a dashi broth, they can be based on either meat, poultry or seafood, or in the interesting example of *chanko nabe*, the traditional robust fare for sumo wrestlers, all three of them!

Donburi comprise another type of one-dish meal, and this name is also used for the deep, covered bowl in which this rice-based dish is usually served. Any of a number of complementary toppings — tempura, teriyaki chicken or steamed sake chicken — can be heaped over a generous serving of rice to make a complete and deliciously satisfying meal.

Some very popular main dishes are actually 'Japanized' versions of foreign dishes. Two of the most favoured, both so often eaten that they are considered virtually a part of Japanese cuisine, are *tonkatsu*, a breaded and fried pork cutlet, and *kare raisu*, Japanese curry with rice.

chicken and vegetable hotpot . . . . serves 4

DIFFERENT FROM THE MORE COMMON STEW-LIKE HOTPOT, THIS CHICKEN AND VEGETABLE RECIPE IS A JUICY DISH MEANT TO BE EATEN ALONGSIDE A BOWL OF RICE. GOBO, LOTUS ROOT AND BAMBOO SHOOTS ARE JUST SEVERAL AMONG ITS MIX OF APPEALING VEGETABLES.

fresh or frozen gobo (burdock root)	100 g (3½ oz)
Japanese rice vinegar	1 teaspoon
fresh or frozen lotus root	100 g (3½ oz)
sesame oil	2 teaspoons
vegetable oil	1 tablespoon
boneless, skinless chicken thighs	750 g (1 lb 10 oz), cut into 3 cm (1¼ in) squares
taro	150 g (5½ oz), peeled and cut into 2 cm (¾ in) squares
carrot	1, cut on the diagonal into 1.5 cm (⅝ in) thick slices
bamboo shoots	100 g (3½ oz) sliced
fresh shiitake mushrooms	100 g (3½ oz), stems discarded, large caps halved
dashi II	500 ml (17 fl oz/2 cups) (see recipe on page 24)
shoyu (Japanese soy sauce)	80 ml (2½ fl oz/⅓ cup)
mirin	60 ml (2 fl oz/¼ cup)
caster (superfine) sugar	1 tablespoon
snow peas (mangetout)	100 g (3½ oz), trimmed
shichimi togarashi (seven-spice mix)	to serve, optional

If using fresh gobo, roughly scrape the skin with a sharp knife, then rinse. Cut into 2 cm (¾ in) pieces on the diagonal. Put in a bowl with 500 ml (17 fl oz/2 cups) water and the vinegar. Leave for about 15 minutes to remove some of the bitterness from the gobo. If using frozen gobo, this step is not necessary as the gobo has been scraped and cut, ready for use.

If using fresh lotus root, peel it, cut into 5 mm (¼ in) slices, then put in cold water. This step is not necessary if using frozen lotus.

Heat the sesame and vegetable oil in a large saucepan over medium–high heat and cook the chicken in batches until lightly golden. Remove from the pan and set aside.

Drain the gobo and lotus. Add the gobo and taro to the pan and cook, stirring frequently, for 2 minutes. Add the lotus and carrot and cook for a further 2 minutes, or until lightly golden. Add the bamboo shoots and shiitake and cook for a further 2 minutes. Pour in the dashi, shoyu and mirin, add the sugar and bring to the boil, then reduce to a simmer. Add the chicken and simmer for a further 10–15 minutes. Just before serving, add the snow peas and stir until just wilted. Serve in deep bowls with rice. Sprinkle with shichimi togarashi, if desired.

Cook the chicken in the sesame and vegetable oil

Add the lotus and carrot and cook for 2 minutes

Just before serving, stir in the snow peas and cook until wilted

chilled soba noodles . . . . serves 4

THIS BUCKWHEAT NOODLE DISH WITH ITS EARTHY FLAVOUR AND SAVOURY DIP IS A HOT WEATHER FAVOURITE IN JAPAN. OFTEN SERVED ON BASKET-WEAVE TRAYS CALLED *ZARU*, THESE COLD NOODLES ARE EQUALLY ATTRACTIVE DISHED UP INTO BOWLS.

dried soba (buckwheat) noodles	250 g (9 oz)
fresh ginger	4 cm (1 1/2 in) piece, cut into thin matchsticks
carrot	1, cut into 4 cm (1 1/2 in) lengths, then cut into thin matchsticks
spring onions (scallions)	4, thinly sliced
nori sheet	1, toasted, cut into thin strips
pickled ginger	to garnish
pickled daikon	thinly sliced, to garnish

dipping sauce

dashi granules	3 tablespoons
shoyu (Japanese soy sauce)	125 ml (4 fl oz/1/2 cup)
mirin	80 ml (2 1/2 fl oz/1/3 cup)

Half-fill a large saucepan with lightly salted water and bring to the boil over high heat, then gradually lower the noodles into the water. Stir so the noodles don't stick together. Pour in 250 ml (9 fl oz/1 cup) cold water and return to the boil. Repeat this step another two to three times, or until the noodles are tender. This cooking method helps to cook this delicate noodle more evenly. The noodles should be *al dente* with no hard core in the centre but not completely soft all the way through. Drain the noodles, then rinse well under cold running water, lightly rubbing the noodles together with your hands to remove any excess starch. Drain thoroughly and set aside.

Bring a saucepan of water to the boil and add the ginger, carrot and spring onion. Blanch for 30 seconds, then drain and put in a bowl of iced water. Drain again when the vegetables are cool.

To make the dipping sauce, combine 375 ml (13 fl oz/1 1/2 cups) water, dashi granules, shoyu, mirin and a good pinch each of salt and pepper in a small pan. Bring to the boil, then cool completely. When ready to serve, pour the sauce into four small, wide bowls.

Toss the noodles and vegetables to combine and arrange in four serving bowls. Scatter the nori strips over the noodles and garnish with a little pickled ginger and daikon. Serve the noodles with the dipping sauce. Dip the noodles into the sauce before eating them.

Toast the nori sheet over low heat for a few seconds

Cut the nori sheet into thin strips using scissors

deep-fried chicken
with seaweed . . . . serves 4

MARINATED NUGGETS OF CHICKEN ARE TREATED TO AN UNCOMMON NORI COATING AND THEN DEEP-FRIED TO A CRISPY GOLDEN BROWN. TASTILY TOPPING A BOWL OF RICE, THIS GINGERY CHICKEN WOULD BE NICELY ACCOMPANIED BY A REFRESHING SALAD OR VEGETABLE DISH.

boneless, skinless chicken breasts	400 g (14 oz)
shoyu (Japanese soy sauce)	60 ml (2 fl oz/¼ cup)
mirin	60 ml (2 fl oz/¼ cup)
fresh ginger	4 cm (1½ in) piece, very finely grated
nori sheet	1, finely chopped or crumbled into very small pieces
cornflour (cornstarch)	40 g (1½ oz/⅓ cup)
vegetable oil	for deep-frying
steamed rice	to serve
pickled ginger	to serve
cucumber	thin slices, to serve

Carefully trim any sinew from the chicken. Cut the chicken into bite-sized pieces and discard any thin ends so that the pieces will be even in size. Place the chicken pieces in a bowl.

Combine the shoyu, mirin and ginger in a small bowl and pour the mixture over the chicken. Toss until the chicken pieces are evenly coated with the marinade. Set aside for 15 minutes, then drain off any excess marinade.

Mix the nori with the cornflour. Using your fingertips, lightly coat each piece of chicken with the cornflour mixture.

Fill a deep-fat fryer or large saucepan one-third full of the oil. Heat to 180°C (350°F), or until a cube of bread dropped into the oil browns in 15 seconds. Add the chicken, six to seven pieces at a time, and fry until golden, turning regularly. Drain on paper towels. Serve with steamed rice, pickled ginger and sliced cucumber.

Nori is a reddish brown marine alga, which is gathered wild as well as cultivated, mainly through the winter season. Dried and cut into crispy, paper-thin sheets, it is usually lightly toasted over a flame to enrich its flavour and colour. Countless billions of sheets of nori are consumed each year by the Japanese. In seaside villages, it is still possible to see hand-gathered, hand-formed nori sheets drying on individual straw mats propped in the sun. Nori is used to wrap *maki-zushi*, *sembei* crackers and *onigiri* rice balls, while flakes and slivers of it flavour and garnish many other dishes. Soy-seasoned nori is often served as an accompaniment to rice at Japanese-style breakfasts.

five-flavoured rice

THIS SATISFYING DISH, CALLED *TAKIKOMI GOHAN* IN JAPANESE, IS POPULAR AND NUTRITIOUS FARE. THE RICE AND ASSORTED ADDED INGREDIENTS, WITH THEIR INDIVIDUAL TEXTURES AND TASTES, ARE COOKED TOGETHER IN SEASONED DASHI TO YIELD A DEEPLY FLAVOURFUL MEAL-IN-A-BOWL.

Japanese short-grain rice	440 g (15½ oz/2 cups)
dried shiitake mushrooms	5
abura-age (deep-fried tofu sheets)	25 g (1 oz)
konnyaku (yam cake)	100 g (3½ oz), optional
carrot	1 small, peeled
bamboo shoots	75 g (2½ oz)
boneless, skinless chicken thighs	500 g (1 lb 2 oz), cut into bite-sized pieces
dashi II	500 ml (17 fl oz/2 cups) (see recipe on page 24)
shoyu (Japanese soy sauce)	80 ml (2½ fl oz/⅓ cup)
mirin	2 tablespoons
mitsuba or flat-leaf (Italian) parsley	2 tablespoons chopped, optional

Rinse the rice several times in cold water until the water runs clear, then soak in fresh water for 1 hour. Meanwhile, soak the shiitake in 375 ml (13 oz/1½ cups) hot water for 30 minutes, then drain well, reserving the liquid. Discard the stems and thinly slice the caps.

Put the abura-age in a heatproof bowl and cover with boiling water for a few minutes. Drain and squeeze the sheets gently between paper towels to remove the excess oil.

Cut the konnyaku, carrot, bamboo shoots and abura-age into 3 cm x 5 mm (1¼ x ¼ in) strips and put in a bowl with the shiitake. Add the chicken pieces to the bowl.

Combine the reserved mushroom liquid, dashi, shoyu, mirin and 1 teaspoon salt in a bowl, then pour the liquid over the chicken and vegetables and set aside for about 20 minutes.

Drain the rice and spread over the base of a large saucepan. Pour the chicken and vegetable mixture over the rice but do not stir. Sit the saucepan over high heat and bring to the boil, then cover, reduce the heat to low and cook for 15 minutes. Turn off the heat, leaving the pan on the stove, and leave to stand for 10 minutes before stirring to combine all the ingredients. If using it, stir in the mitsuba and serve.

Pour the liquid over the abura-age, vegetables and chicken

Top the rice with the chicken and vegetable mixture

Stir the rice after it has been left to stand for 10 minutes

tonkatsu

. . . . serves 4

ALTHOUGH TONKATSU ACTUALLY COUNTS AS *YOSHOKU*, A WESTERN DISH, SINCE IT WAS FIRST TASTED IN THE LATE 19TH CENTURY, THE JAPANESE HAVE ADOPTED IT AS THEIR OWN. THEIR VERSION HAS A CRISP, LIGHT PANKO CRUST, AND IS SERVED SLICED TO ENABLE EATING WITH CHOPSTICKS.

pork schnitzels	4 x 150 g (5½ oz) or 700 g (1 lb 9 oz) pork fillets
plain (all-purpose) flour	for coating
egg	1, lightly beaten
panko (Japanese breadcrumbs)	for coating
vegetable oil	for deep-frying
sesame oil	60 ml (2 fl oz/¼ cup)
white cabbage	¼, very finely shredded
lemon wedges	to serve
Japanese mustard	to serve, optional

tonkatsu sauce

worcestershire sauce	60 ml (2 fl oz/¼ cup)
tamari or shoyu (Japanese soy sauce)	2 tablespoons
caster (superfine) sugar	2 tablespoons
tomato sauce (ketchup)	2 tablespoons
Japanese mustard	½ teaspoon
sake	1 tablespoon
Japanese rice vinegar	1 tablespoon
garlic	1 clove, bruised

Using a meat mallet or the back of a large, heavy knife, pound the pork schnitzel until 5 mm (¼ in) thick, then lightly score around the edges with the point of the knife to prevent it from curling during cooking. If using pork fillets, trim off any skinny ends and cut into 5 cm (2 in) lengths — do not pound.

Season the flour with salt and pepper. Lightly coat the pork with the seasoned flour. Dip the pork pieces into the egg, allowing any excess to drip off, then coat in the panko, pressing down on both sides to help the crumbs adhere. Transfer to a plate, cover and refrigerate for 15 minutes.

Meanwhile, to make the tonkatsu sauce, combine all the ingredients in a small saucepan and bring to the boil over high heat. Reduce to a simmer and cook for 20 minutes, or until glossy and thickened slightly.

Fill a deep heavy-based saucepan or deep-fat fryer one-third full of vegetable oil and add the sesame oil. Heat to 170°C (325°F), or until a cube of bread dropped into the oil browns in 20 seconds. Cook the schnitzels one at a time, or the fillet a few pieces at a time, turning once or twice for about 4 minutes, or until golden brown all over and cooked through. The fillet will take a little longer, about 6–8 minutes. Drain on crumpled paper towels, then keep warm in a low oven while you cook the rest.

Slice the pork schnitzel, then lift it onto serving plates, arranging the fillet in its original shape. Serve with a pile of cabbage and lemon wedges, and pass around the sauce. If you like, serve with mustard. For a hearty meal, serve with rice and miso soup (see recipe on page 36).

Coat the pork with the panko, pressing down on the crumbs

Cook the schnitzels, one at a time, until golden brown

glazed beef and vegetable rolls

THE CLASSIC IDEA OF 'MEAT AND VEGETABLES' IS REDEFINED BY THESE FLAVOURFUL ROLLS. ASPARAGUS SPEARS AND SPRING ONION (SCALLION) STALKS ARE WRAPPED IN THIN SLICES OF BEEF, BROWNED IN A LITTLE OIL, AND ENRICHED WITH A SLIGHTLY SWEET SOY GLAZE.

sirloin steak	400 g (14 oz), cut into 3 cm (1 1/4 in) thick slices, trimmed
potato starch	2 1/2 teaspoons, for sprinkling
spring onions (scallions)	6, cut into twelve 6 cm (2 1/2 in) lengths
asparagus spears	6 thin, trimmed, cut in half and lightly blanched
vegetable oil	for cooking
sake	80 ml (2 1/2 fl oz/1/3 cup)
mirin	80 ml (2 1/2 fl oz/1/3 cup)
shoyu (Japanese soy sauce)	80 ml (2 1/2 fl oz/1/3 cup)
caster (superfine) sugar	1 1/2 tablespoons

Freeze the beef for 3 hours, or until partially frozen. Use a sharp knife to slice very thinly along the length of the steak to make long, thin strips — you should have about 24 slices. Lay one strip of beef on a clean work surface with the short end towards you. Lay another strip alongside it so that it just overlaps along its length, forming one strip of meat about 6 cm (2 1/2 in) wide at the short end. Sprinkle with a little seasoned potato starch. Repeat with the rest of the meat — you should have 12 strips in total. Put a piece of spring onion and asparagus along the edge of the beef closest to you, then roll up and secure with kitchen string. Repeat with the remaining beef and vegetables.

Heat a little vegetable oil in a large frying pan over medium–high heat, then, working in batches, cook the rolls for 5–7 minutes, or until browned all over. Remove from the pan.

Combine the sake, mirin, shoyu and caster sugar with 80 ml (2 1/2 fl oz/1/3 cup) water, then add to the pan, stirring until the sugar dissolves. Bring to the boil for 1 minute, then reduce to a simmer. Add the beef rolls and cook for 5 minutes, or until cooked through, turning occasionally. Remove from the pan. Carefully cut the string from the rolls, transfer the beef rolls to a plate, cover with foil and set aside until needed.

Pour any meat juices from the resting meat into the pan, then sit the pan over medium–high heat and bring to the boil. Cook for 5–7 minutes, or until the liquid is slightly thickened and glossy. Immediately return the beef rolls to the pan and cook for a further minute, turning continuously to coat and glaze well. Remove from the heat. Cut each roll into thirds if serving with chopsticks, and drizzle with the remaining glaze before serving immediately. Serve with a crisp green salad and rice.

Slice the partially frozen steak into very thin strips

Roll up the beef to enclose the vegetables and secure with string

scallops with soba noodles and dashi broth .... serves 4

AS DELICIOUS AS A SIMPLE BOWL OF BUCKWHEAT NOODLES IN BROTH CAN BE, THE ADDITION OF LIGHTLY COOKED FRESH SCALLOPS AND ASIAN BLACK FUNGUS TURN IT INTO A SUBSTANTIAL MEAL. SLIVERS OF SHREDDED NORI PROVIDE AN ELEGANT GARNISH.

dried soba (buckwheat) noodles	250 g (9 oz)
mirin	3 tablespoons
shoyu (Japanese soy sauce)	60 ml (2 fl oz/¼ cup)
rice wine vinegar	2 teaspoons
dashi granules	1 teaspoon
spring onions (scallions)	2, sliced on the diagonal
fresh ginger	1 teaspoon finely chopped
scallops	24 large, roe removed
fresh black fungus	5, chopped (see note)
nori sheet	1, shredded

Cook the soba noodles in a large saucepan of boiling water for 5 minutes, or until tender. Drain and rinse under cold water.

Put the mirin, shoyu, vinegar, dashi granules and 750 ml (26 fl oz/ 3 cups) water in a saucepan. Bring to the boil, then reduce the heat and simmer for 3–4 minutes. Add the spring onion and ginger and keep at a gentle simmer until needed.

Heat a chargrill pan or plate until very hot and sear the scallops on both sides, in batches, for 1 minute. Remove.

Divide the noodles and black fungus among four deep serving bowls. Pour 185 ml (6 fl oz/¾ cup) broth into each bowl and top with six scallops each. Garnish with the shredded nori and serve.

Note: If fresh black fungus is not available, use dried instead. Soak in warm water for 15–20 minutes before use.

Soba means buckwheat in Japanese, but is also the name for buckwheat noodles, which is the primary way this grain is utilized in Japan. Because buckwheat has no gluten content, wheat flour and/or wild yam is commonly added to the noodle dough to help bind it. The natural colour of soba noodles is pale brown, although they are sometimes flavoured and coloured with green tea. *Kake soba* is served in a bowl with a hot soy sauce-based broth, with many variations in toppings. Often served cold on a basket tray or bamboo mat in summer, *zaru soba* is presented with a dipping sauce called *tsuyu*, seasoned with spring onions (scallions) and wasabi.

three ways with sauces

JAPANESE SAUCES ARE TYPICALLY LIGHT, AND ARE APPLIED WITH A LIGHT HAND TOO. SOY SAUCE OR SEASONED VARIATIONS OF IT, SUCH AS TEMPURA SAUCE OR PONZU SAUCE, ARE THIN AND USUALLY USED FOR DIPPING. DRESSINGS BASED ON RICE VINEGAR ARE GENERALLY ALSO THIN. SAUCES THICKENED WITH SESAME SEEDS, NUTS, MISO PASTE OR TOFU ARE SOMETIMES SERVED ATOP SALADS AND SIMMERED DISHES. SAUCES NEVER OVERWHELM THE NATURAL FLAVOURS AND TEXTURES OF THE FOODS THEMSELVES, BUT SERVE AS AN ACCENT TO THEM.

ponzu

Put 1 tablespoon lemon juice, 1 tablespoon lime juice, 1 tablespoon rice vinegar, 60 ml (2 fl oz/$\frac{1}{4}$ cup) shoyu (Japanese soy sauce), 1 tablespoon mirin, 60 ml (2 fl oz/$\frac{1}{4}$ cup) sake, 1 teaspoon sugar and 1 tablespoon katsuobushi (bonito flakes) in a non-metallic bowl. Wipe a 4 cm (1$\frac{1}{2}$ in) square piece of konbu (kelp) with a damp cloth, cut it into strips and add to the bowl. Stir to combine the ingredients and to dissolve the sugar. Cover with plastic wrap and refrigerate for 24 hours. Strain through muslin (cheesecloth) or a fine sieve before using. Makes about 250 ml (9 fl oz/1 cup).

sesame seed sauce

Toast 100 g (3$\frac{1}{2}$ oz/$\frac{2}{3}$ cup) sesame seeds in a dry frying pan over medium heat for 3–4 minutes, shaking the pan gently, until the seeds are golden brown. Remove from the pan at once to prevent burning. Grind the seeds using a mortar and pestle or a *suribachi* (Japanese ribbed mortar) until a paste is formed. Add 2 teaspoons oil, if necessary, to assist in forming a paste. Mix the paste with 125 ml (4 fl oz/$\frac{1}{2}$ cup) shoyu (Japanese soy sauce), 2 tablespoons mirin, 3 teaspoons caster (superfine) sugar, $\frac{1}{2}$ teaspoon dashi granules and 125 ml (4 fl oz/$\frac{1}{2}$ cup) warm water. Store, covered, in the refrigerator and use within 2 days of preparation. Makes about 435 ml (15$\frac{1}{4}$ fl oz/1$\frac{3}{4}$ cups).

tempura dipping sauce

Combine 310 ml (10$\frac{3}{4}$ fl oz/1$\frac{1}{4}$ cups) dashi II (see recipe on page 24), 60 ml (2 fl oz/$\frac{1}{4}$ cup) mirin and 80 ml (2$\frac{1}{2}$ fl oz/$\frac{1}{3}$ cup) shoyu (Japanese soy sauce) in a small saucepan and bring to the boil over high heat. Reduce the heat to low and keep warm until ready to serve. Makes 685 ml (23$\frac{1}{2}$ fl oz/2$\frac{3}{4}$ cups).

clockwise from front: ponzu, sesame seed sauce, tempura dipping sauce

okinawan
slow-cooked pork

serves 4–6

PORK IS EXTREMELY POPULAR ON THE ISLANDS OF OKINAWA, WHERE THE CULTURE AND CUISINE HAVE BEEN INFLUENCED BY THEIR PROXIMITY TO CHINA. THIS TENDER, SUCCULENT, GINGER-FLAVOURED DISH IS SLOW-COOKED FOR SEVERAL HOURS, AND BLACK SUGAR LENDS A PARTICULARLY CARAMELY GLAZE.

vegetable oil	2 teaspoons
pork belly	1 kg (2 lb 4 oz) boneless, cut into 5 cm (2 in) cubes
fresh ginger	100 g (3½ oz), peeled and cut into thick slices
dashi II	500 ml (17 fl oz/2 cups) (see recipe on page 24)
sake	170 ml (5½ fl oz/⅔ cup)
mirin	60 ml (2 fl oz/¼ cup)
black or dark brown sugar	80 g (2¾ oz/⅓ cup firmly packed)
shoyu (Japanese soy sauce)	125 ml (4 fl oz/½ cup)
Japanese mustard	to serve, optional

Heat the oil in a large, heavy-based saucepan or small flameproof casserole dish over high heat. Add the pork in two batches and cook for 5 minutes, or until browned all over.

Rinse the pork under hot water to remove excess oil. Remove any excess fat from the pan and return the pork to the pan, adding enough cold water to cover well. Add the ginger slices and bring to the boil over high heat. Reduce to a simmer and cook for 2 hours. Top up with water if needed. Strain, discarding the liquid and ginger. Set the pork aside.

Put the dashi, sake, mirin, sugar and shoyu in a clean heavy-based saucepan and stir over high heat until the sugar has dissolved. Add the pork and return to the boil, then reduce to a simmer and cook, turning occasionally, for 1 hour, or until the pork is very tender. Remove from the heat and leave the pork to rest in the liquid for 20 minutes. Place the pork in a serving dish, cover and keep warm while you reduce the sauce.

Sit the saucepan over high heat, bring the liquid to the boil and cook for 5 minutes, or until the sauce has reduced to a slightly syrupy glaze. Return the pork to the sauce and stir to combine before arranging in a serving dish. Pour over any remaining sauce and serve immediately, with a little Japanese mustard on the side, if using. Serve with rice and Asian greens.

Brown the pork belly pieces in two batches

Rinse the pork with hot water to remove any excess oil

Heat the dashi mixture in the pan, then add the pork

sake-glazed salmon .... serves 4

BOTH SAVOURY AND SWEET OFTEN MINGLE IN JAPANESE CUISINE. THESE TENDER AND JUICY SALMON SLICES ARE
SERVED WITH A LIGHTLY SWEETENED SOY SAUCE AND BUTTER GLAZE. SERVE WITH A VEGETABLE SIDE DISH AND
A BOWL OF STEAMED RICE.

salmon fillets	4 x 175 g (6 oz)
vegetable oil	1 tablespoon
sesame oil	1 teaspoon
unsalted butter	40 g (1 1/2 oz)
sake	60 ml (2 fl oz/1/4 cup)
shoyu (Japanese soy sauce)	1 1/2 tablespoons
mirin	1 tablespoon
caster (superfine) sugar	2 teaspoons
fresh ginger	1/4 teaspoon finely grated

Check the salmon carefully for bones, pulling out any you find
with clean tweezers. Season lightly with salt.

Heat the oils in a large, heavy-based frying pan over medium–high
heat. Add the salmon pieces, skin side down, and cook for
3 minutes, or until the skin is golden. Reduce the heat to medium,
turn the fish over and cook for a further 2–3 minutes, or until
almost cooked through. Remove the salmon from the pan, cover
and set aside.

Remove any excess oil from the pan, then add the butter, sake,
shoyu, mirin, sugar and ginger to the pan. Increase the heat to
high and stir to dissolve the sugar. Bring to the boil and cook,
stirring, for 2 minutes, or until slightly thickened. Drizzle the glaze
over the salmon.

Salmon, called *sake* in Japanese,
is appreciated for its fine flavour
and also for its attractive colour,
which adds to the visual appeal
— essential in a Japanese meal.
This lovely firm-fleshed fish of
rivers and oceans appears in
many ways on the Japanese
table. Japan is, in fact, the
largest market in the world for
salmon. The steaks or fillets are
sometimes prepared teriyaki-
style or sautéed in butter, and
included in mixed fish hotpots.
Salmon can also be served as
sashimi and the roe is also
sometimes enjoyed. *Shiozake*,
salt salmon, is popular grilled
(broiled), although it is too salty
for some tastes.

poached pork
with miso sauce .... serves 4

PORK FILLET POACHED IN A DASHI AND VEGETABLE BROTH YIELDS TENDER SLICES OF PORK, WHICH ARE SERVED
ATOP A JULIENNE OF CRISPY VEGETABLES. SOME OF THE FLAVOUR-FILLED POACHING LIQUID IS INCORPORATED
INTO THE SAUCE, WHICH IS MADE FROM TWO KINDS OF MISO.

dashi II	2 litres (70 fl oz/8 cups) (see recipe on page 24)
carrot	1, peeled and chopped
celery	1 stalk, chopped
spring onions (scallions)	6, chopped
fresh ginger	10 x 2 cm (4 x 3/4 in) piece, thickly sliced
pork loin fillet	1 kg (2 lb 4 oz)

salad

Lebanese (short) cucumbers	2
daikon	180 g (6 1/2 oz), about 12 cm (4 1/2 in) in length, peeled
celery	1 stalk
spring onions (scallions)	3

miso sauce

red miso paste	2 tablespoons
white miso paste	2 tablespoons
sake	2 tablespoons
sesame oil	1 teaspoon
caster (superfine) sugar	2 tablespoons
garlic	2 cloves, crushed

Combine the dashi, carrot, celery, spring onion and ginger in a saucepan just large enough to fit the piece of pork. Sit the pan over high heat and bring the liquid to the boil. Meanwhile, tie the pork with string to help keep its shape.

Lower the pork into the stock, return the stock to the boil, then reduce to a simmer and cook, turning the pork occasionally, for 40–45 minutes, or until the meat is evenly cooked through and tender. Remove the pan from the heat and allow the pork to cool slightly in the liquid. Transfer the pork to a bowl, then strain the stock over the pork. Cover and refrigerate until chilled.

To make the salad, cut the cucumbers, daikon, celery and spring onions into 6 cm (2 1/2 in) lengths. Cut into thin strips or julienne.

Remove the pork from the poaching liquid and reserve 60 ml (2 fl oz/1/4 cup) of the liquid. Freeze the remaining liquid for use as a soup base or discard.

To make the miso sauce, combine all the ingredients and the reserved poaching liquid in a bowl and stir until smooth. Slice the pork and serve over the salad with the sauce drizzled over.

Tie the pork fillet with kitchen string to help hold its shape

Lower the pork into the dashi stock and return to the boil

To make the miso sauce, combine the ingredients in a small bowl

omelettes filled
with rice

YOSHOKU MEANS 'WESTERN FOOD' BUT IT ACTUALLY REFERS TO THOSE NEW DISHES OF THE LATE 19TH AND EARLY 20TH CENTURIES, WHICH THE JAPANESE ADAPTED TO SUIT THEMSELVES. AMONG THEM IS *OMURAISU*, A SOY- AND MIRIN-SEASONED OMELETTE WRAPPED AROUND FLAVOURED RICE.

Japanese short-grain rice	275 g (9³/4 oz/1¹/4 cups)
butter	25 g (1 oz)
sesame oil	a few drops
onion	1, finely chopped
garlic	2 cloves, crushed
fresh ginger	2 teaspoons finely chopped
boneless, skinless chicken thighs	250 g (9 oz), diced
peas	50 g (1³/4 oz/¹/3 cup) frozen, thawed
tomato sauce (ketchup)	125 ml (4 fl oz/¹/2 cup), plus extra to serve
Japanese mayonnaise	to serve, optional

omelettes

eggs	8
shoyu (Japanese soy sauce)	2 teaspoons
mirin	1 tablespoon
caster (superfine) sugar	1 teaspoon

Rinse the rice several times in cold water until the water runs clear, then drain in a colander for 1 hour. Put in a saucepan with 375 ml (13 fl oz/1¹/2 cups) water. Bring to the boil, then cover with a tight-fitting lid, reduce the heat to low and simmer for 15 minutes. Turn off the heat but leave the pan on the hotplate. Working quickly, remove the lid, lay a clean tea towel (dish towel) over the top, then put the lid on and set aside for 15 minutes. Cool completely, then rinse well.

Melt the butter in a large frying pan, add the sesame oil and onion and cook over medium heat for 8–10 minutes, or until golden. Add the garlic, ginger and diced chicken and cook, stirring, for 1 minute, or until the chicken starts to change colour. Add the peas and tomato sauce and mix well. Add the rice and mix again until the rice is evenly pink from the tomato sauce. Continue cooking, stirring occasionally, for about 5 minutes, or until the chicken is cooked and the rice is completely heated through. Season, then cover and set aside while you make the omelettes.

Lightly oil a Japanese omelette pan or non-stick frying pan and put over medium heat. Combine all the omelette ingredients in a bowl and lightly beat. Pour one-quarter of the egg mixture into the pan. Using chopsticks or a soft spatula, gently drag the outside edges of the egg into the centre until it just starts to set, then leave to cook for 1 minute. Spoon a quarter of the rice mixture along the centre line of the egg, then very carefully fold two sides towards the centre, over the rice, so you have a rectangular omelette. Put a serving plate over the top and very carefully invert the omelette onto the plate so the seam is on the bottom.

Repeat with the remaining mixture to make three more omelettes. Serve with extra tomato sauce and a little mayonnaise, if you like.

salmon and tofu balls ....makes 18

MOIST AND CRISPY, THESE DEEP-FRIED CROQUETTE-LIKE MORSELS OF RED SALMON ARE LIGHTENED WITH MASHED TOFU. SERVED WITH COMPLEMENTARY SIDES, THEY MAKE A LIGHT MAIN DISH, BUT WOULD ALSO BE AN APPETIZING STARTER OR AN ACCOMPANIMENT TO SAKE.

wasabi mayonnaise dipping sauce

Japanese mayonnaise	125 g (4 1/2 oz/1/2 cup)
shoyu (Japanese soy sauce)	1 teaspoon
mirin	1 teaspoon
Japanese rice vinegar	1 teaspoon
wasabi paste	1/2 teaspoon

salmon and tofu balls

silken firm tofu	200 g (7 oz)
red salmon	400 g (14 oz) tinned, well drained to yield about 250 g (9 oz)
spring onions (scallions)	2, finely chopped
fresh ginger	2 teaspoons finely grated, squeezed to remove excess liquid
garlic	1 clove, crushed
mirin	2 teaspoons
shoyu (Japanese soy sauce)	1 tablespoon
egg	1
plain (all-purpose) flour	2 tablespoons
ground white pepper	pinch
vegetable oil	for deep-frying
potato starch	for coating
lemon wedges	to serve

To make the wasabi mayonnaise dipping sauce, put all the ingredients in a small bowl and combine well.

To weight the tofu, wrap it in a clean tea towel (dish towel). Put two plates on top of the tofu and leave for about 2 hours to extract any excess moisture. Remove from the tea towel, then pat dry with paper towels. Put in a bowl and finely mash with a fork. Break up the salmon with a fork, picking out any bones. Finely mash with a fork and add to the bowl with the tofu, along with the spring onion, ginger, garlic, mirin, shoyu, egg and flour and combine well. Season with salt and white pepper. If the mixture is still too wet, put in a fine colander and leave for 30 minutes to drain out the excess liquid. With clean hands, form into balls about the size of a walnut and set aside — you should get about 18 balls. Don't worry if the balls seem quite soft.

Fill a deep-fat fryer or large saucepan one-third full of oil and heat to 180°C (350°F), or until a cube of bread dropped into the oil browns in 15 seconds. Lightly coat the balls with potato starch, then immediately lower into the hot oil. Cook in batches, turning occasionally, for 2–3 minutes, or until golden all over and cooked through. Drain on paper towels and keep warm in a low oven while you repeat with the remaining mixture. Serve immediately with lemon wedges and the dipping sauce.

Add the finely mashed salmon to the bowl of mashed tofu

Coat the salmon and tofu balls with potato starch

Lower the balls into the hot oil, cooking them in batches

japanese fried rice .... serves 4

CALLED *YAKIMESHI* OR *CHAHAN* IN JAPAN, WHERE IT IS PARTICULARLY POPULAR AMONG THE YOUNGER GENERATIONS, FRIED RICE IS ACTUALLY A CHINESE-STYLE DISH. IT'S AN ENTICING WAY TO USE UP LEFTOVER RICE AND WHATEVER ELSE MIGHT BE ON HAND IN THE REFRIGERATOR AND PANTRY.

Japanese short-grain rice	275 g (9³/4 oz/1¹/4 cups)
eggs	2
dashi II	2 tablespoons
	(see recipe on page 24)
sake	2 teaspoons
sugar	1 teaspoon
ground white pepper	pinch
shoyu (Japanese soy sauce)	1 tablespoon
vegetable oil	for pan-frying
sesame oil	2 teaspoons
spring onions (scallions)	3, 2 chopped, 1 sliced on the diagonal
fresh shiitake mushrooms	4, stems discarded, caps sliced
bamboo shoots	50 g (1³/4 oz), thinly sliced
sliced ham	50 g (1³/4 oz), cut into strips
green peas	40 g (1¹/2 oz/¹/4 cup) frozen, thawed
pickled ginger	1 teaspoon finely chopped

Rinse the rice several times in cold water until the water runs clear, then drain in a colander for 1 hour. Put in a saucepan with 375 ml (13 fl oz/1¹/2 cups) water. Bring to the boil, then cover with a tight-fitting lid, reduce the heat to low and simmer for 15 minutes. Turn off the heat but leave the pan on the hotplate. Working quickly, remove the lid, lay a clean tea towel (dish towel) over the top, then put the lid on and set aside for 15 minutes. Cool completely, then rinse well.

Put the eggs, dashi, sake, sugar, white pepper and 2 teaspoons of the shoyu in a bowl and mix well. Heat a little of the vegetable oil in a small non-stick frying pan over medium heat, then pour in the egg mixture. Drag the egg mixture into the centre of the pan with a wooden spoon a couple of times, and allow the mixture to flow back to the edges. Cook for 1 minute, or until almost set, then flip over and cook for a further 30 seconds. Remove and allow to cool. Roll the omelette up, then slice thinly.

Pour a little more vegetable oil and half the sesame oil into a wok or large frying pan and heat over medium heat. Add the chopped spring onion, shiitake and bamboo shoots. Stir-fry for 2 minutes, then add the ham and peas and stir-fry for a further 2 minutes. Remove from the wok.

Add a little more vegetable oil and the remaining sesame oil to the wok and add the rice. Stir-fry for 2 minutes, then return the mushroom mixture to the wok, along with the remaining shoyu and the pickled ginger and stir to combine and heat through. Scoop into a bowl and top with the egg and remaining sliced spring onion. Serve immediately.

sesame tuna steaks
with nori rice..serves 4

TUNA, SO TASTY WHEN SERVED AS SASHIMI OR AS A SUSHI TOPPING, IS ALSO VERY DELICIOUS COOKED. THESE STEAKS, COATED WITH CRUNCHY SESAME SEEDS, ARE SAUTEED ONLY UNTIL THE CRUST IS GOLDEN, BRINGING OUT THE NUTTY AROMA WHILE LEAVING THE TUNA RARE.

tuna steaks	4 x 200 g (7 oz)
sesame seeds	115 g (4 oz/3/4 cup)
medium-grain rice	200 g (7 oz/1 cup)
rice wine vinegar	2 1/2 tablespoons
mirin	1 tablespoon
sugar	1 teaspoon
nori sheet	1, finely shredded
peanut oil	60 ml (2 fl oz/1/4 cup)
Japanese or whole-egg mayonnaise	125 g (4 1/2 oz/1/2 cup)
wasabi paste	2 teaspoons
pickled ginger	to serve, optional

Coat the tuna steaks in the sesame seeds, pressing down to coat well. Refrigerate until needed.

Wash the rice until the water runs clear, then put in a saucepan with 500 ml (17 fl oz/2 cups) water. Bring to the boil, then reduce the heat to very low and cook, covered, for 10–12 minutes. Turn off the heat and leave, covered, for 5 minutes. While hot, pour on the combined rice wine vinegar, mirin, sugar and 1/4 teaspoon salt. Stir with a fork to separate the grains, then fold in the shredded nori. Keep warm.

Heat the oil in a large frying pan, add the tuna steaks and cook for 1–2 minutes on each side, or until the sesame seeds are crisp and golden. The tuna should still be a little pink in the middle. Drain on paper towels.

Spoon the rice into four lightly greased 125 ml (4 fl oz/1/2 cup) ramekins or cups, pressing down lightly, then invert onto each plate and remove the ramekins. Combine the mayonnaise and wasabi in a small bowl. Serve the tuna with the nori rice and with some wasabi mayonnaise on the side. Garnish with pickled ginger, if desired.

Press down on the sesame seeds so they adhere to the tuna

Fry the sesame-coated tuna until the seeds are golden

Spoon the nori rice into four lightly greased ramekins or cups

shabu-shabu..serves 4

INSPIRED BY MONGOLIAN HOTPOT COOKERY, SHABU-SHABU IS ONE OF THE MOST ENJOYABLE OF WINTER DISHES. THE ARRAY OF INGREDIENTS IS PREPARED IN ADVANCE, MAKING IT POSSIBLE FOR THE HOSTS TO RELAX AND ENJOY A CONVIVIAL MEAL WITH THEIR GUESTS.

scotch fillet (rib eye)	750 g (1 lb 10 oz), partially frozen
spring onions (scallions)	15
carrots	3
button mushrooms	400 g (14 oz)
Chinese cabbage	1/2
firm (cotton) tofu	150 g (51/2 oz)
ready-made shabu-shabu sauce	to serve (or sesame seed sauce, see recipe on page 131)
Japanese short-grain rice	220 g (7 oz/1 cup), cooked
chicken stock	2 litres (70 fl oz/8 cups) (see notes)

Cut the steak into very thin slices and set aside. Cut the firm section of the spring onions into 4 cm (1½ in) lengths and discard the dark green tops. Slice the carrots very thinly. Slice the mushrooms. Chop the cabbage into bite-sized pieces and discard any tough parts. Cut the tofu into bite-sized cubes.

Arrange the prepared vegetables, tofu and meat in separate piles on a serving platter. Cover with plastic wrap and refrigerate until about 30 minutes before cooking time.

Set the table with individual place settings, each with a serving bowl, a bowl of shabu-shabu sauce, a bowl of rice, chopsticks, soup spoons (if desired) and napkins. Position the serving platter and cooking vessel (see notes) so they are within easy reach of each diner. When all the diners are seated, pour the stock into the cooking vessel, cover and bring to a simmer. Each diner then picks up an ingredient or two with their chopsticks, and places it in the simmering stock for about 1 minute, or until just cooked. (Do not overcook — the vegetables should be just tender and the steak still pink in the centre.) The food is then dipped into the sauce and eaten with the rice. The remaining stock can be served as soup at the end of the meal.

Notes: Dashi, made from dashi granules, can be substituted for the chicken stock. Use an electric wok, a frying pan or flameproof casserole dish on a burner, or a steamboat to cook this dish.

Use a heavy knife to thickly slice the cabbage

Cut the slices into smaller pieces, discarding any tough parts

Cut the block of tofu into bite-sized cubes

simmered chicken meatballs . . . . serves 4

CLASSIC JAPANESE SEASONING INGREDIENTS SUCH AS SAKE, SOY SAUCE AND MIRIN, ALONG WITH THE AROMATIC FLAVOURS OF FRESH GINGER AND SESAME OIL INFUSE THESE SIMMERED CHICKEN MEATBALLS. THE MEATBALLS ARE SERVED IN A SAUCE, WHICH HAS BEEN SLIGHTLY THICKENED BY THE ADDITION OF KUZU, A TYPE OF STARCH.

boneless, skinless chicken thighs	300 g (10½ oz)
spring onions (scallions)	3, 2 chopped, 1 thinly sliced
fresh ginger	1 teaspoon finely grated, and its juice
egg	1
sake	1 teaspoon
shoyu (Japanese soy sauce)	1 tablespoon
mirin	1 teaspoon
panko (Japanese breadcrumbs)	20 g (¾ oz/⅓ cup)
sesame oil	1 teaspoon
vegetable oil	1 tablespoon

sauce

dashi II	500 ml (17 fl oz/2 cups) (see recipe on page 24)
mirin	80 ml (2½ fl oz/⅓ cup)
sake	60 ml (2 fl oz/¼ cup)
konbu (kelp)	4 cm (1½ in) length, wiped with a damp cloth, and cut into 1 cm (½ in) strips
shoyu (Japanese soy sauce)	1½ tablespoons
kuzu starch or arrowroot	1 teaspoon

Put the chicken in a food processor and process until roughly minced (ground). Add the chopped spring onion, ginger and ginger juice, egg, sake, shoyu and mirin and process until finely chopped. Transfer to a bowl and add the panko, mixing well with your hands to combine. Cover and refrigerate for 1 hour. Roll into balls about 3 cm (1¼ in) in diameter.

Heat the oils in a non-stick frying pan over medium heat and add the balls in batches. Cook for 5 minutes, or until golden all over. Remove the pan from the heat.

Combine all the sauce ingredients, except the kuzu, in a saucepan and bring to the boil over high heat. Remove the konbu and discard. Add the chicken balls and return the sauce to the boil, then reduce to a simmer and cook for 5 minutes, or until cooked through. Remove the balls with a slotted spoon and set aside.

Mix the kuzu with a little of the hot liquid in a small bowl to form a loose paste, then stir into the pan — stir over high heat until the sauce boils and thickens to a light coating consistency. Place the chicken balls in a serving bowl and pour the sauce over. Garnish with the thinly sliced spring onion.

Use your hands to combine the panko and chicken mixture

Cook the chicken balls in the hot oil until golden

Add the browned chicken balls to the sauce

perfect sashimi

This Japanese delicacy uses only the freshest, finest fish, served thinly sliced and eaten raw. So as not to overpower the delicate flavour and texture, sashimi is served with only a dipping sauce and an elegant garnish of shiso leaves, shredded daikon or carrot. Various fish and shellfish are used to make sashimi, all served raw, with the exception of octopus. Sashimi is usually served as a first course, before the palate is tainted by other foods and flavours.

To make the sashimi, first trim any skin, bloodline or dark flesh from 450 g (1 lb) of the finest sashimi-grade tuna or salmon fillet. Cut the fish along its length into two even blocks, then cut each block into rectangles 6 cm (2½ in) wide. Cut each rectangle into 5–10 mm (¼–½ in) slices across the width. You should get at least 30 slices.

Divide the sashimi slices among four platters in an overlapping row. Add a mound of finely julienned daikon and serve with shoyu (Japanese soy sauce), wasabi paste and pickled ginger on the side. Guests should use chopsticks to mix a little wasabi paste or fresh ginger into the shoyu or simply smear a little of the wasabi onto the fish itself and dip into the shoyu — it should not be dunked, as the strong flavour of the shoyu will overpower the delicate flavour of the raw fish. Pickled ginger will refresh the palate. Serves 4.

steak in roasted
sesame seed marinade .... serves 4

THE RICH ESSENCE OF A SESAME AND SOY MARINADE SPIKED WITH GINGER AND GARLIC PERMEATES THESE JUICY STEAKS. A HEAP OF CRISP SPRING ONION (SCALLION) CURLS MAKES AN ATTRACTIVE GARNISH, WHILE A SPICY DIPPING SAUCE ADDS STILL MORE FLAVOUR AT THE TABLE.

sesame seeds	2 tablespoons
garlic	1 clove, crushed
fresh ginger	3 cm (1 1/4 in) piece, grated
shoyu (Japanese soy sauce)	2 tablespoons
sake	1 tablespoon
caster (superfine) sugar	1 teaspoon
scotch fillet (rib eye)	500 g (1 lb 2 oz), cut into 4 steaks
spring onions (scallions)	3
oil	1 tablespoon

dipping sauce

fresh ginger	4 cm (1 1/2 in) piece
shichimi togarashi (seven-spice mix)	1/2 teaspoon
shoyu (Japanese soy sauce)	125 ml (4 fl oz/1/2 cup)
dashi granules	2 teaspoons

Roast the sesame seeds in a dry frying pan over low heat for 2 minutes, shaking the pan constantly, until the seeds begin to pop. Crush the toasted seeds in a mortar and pestle.

Place the crushed sesame seeds, garlic, ginger, shoyu, sake and sugar in a bowl and whisk until the sugar has dissolved. Place the steaks in a shallow dish, spoon the marinade over the top and marinate for 30 minutes.

To make the dipping sauce, cut the ginger lengthways into very fine strips about 4 cm (1 1/2 in) long. Put the sliced ginger, shichimi togarashi, shoyu, dashi and 2 tablespoons water in a small bowl and whisk lightly until well combined.

Cut the spring onions lengthways into very fine strips about 4 cm (1 1/2 in) long. Place the strips in a bowl of iced water and leave until they are crisp and curled, then drain.

Remove the steaks from the marinade and lightly brush them with the oil. Grill (broil) or fry them in a frying pan or chargrill pan for 4–6 minutes on each side — don't overcook or they will become tough. Set the steaks aside for 5 minutes, then cut into diagonal slices. Arrange the slices on serving plates and drizzle over a little of the dipping sauce. Garnish with the spring onion curls and serve with steamed rice and the remaining dipping sauce.

Whisk the sesame seed mixture to dissolve the sugar

Put the spring onion strips in a bowl of iced water until they curl

Cook the steaks for 4–6 minutes on each side

steamed sake chicken .... serves 4

ALTHOUGH GRAPE WINE IS MORE FAMILIAR TO MOST WESTERN COOKS, SAKE, JAPAN'S BELOVED RICE BREW, CAN BE A WONDERFUL MARINADE BASE. ENHANCED WITH A VARIETY OF ASIAN SEASONINGS, IT GIVES THESE STEAMED CHICKEN BREASTS A PARTICULARLY INVITING TENDERNESS AND FLAVOUR.

chicken breasts	500 g (1 lb 2 oz) with skin on
sake	80 ml (2 1/2 fl oz/1/3 cup)
lemon juice	2 tablespoons
fresh ginger	4 cm (1 1/2 in) piece, thinly sliced
shoyu (Japanese soy sauce)	2 tablespoons
mirin	1 tablespoon
sesame oil	1 teaspoon
spring onion (scallion)	1, sliced on the diagonal, plus extra to garnish
red capsicum (pepper)	1/2 small, skin removed, flesh cut into thin 3 cm (1 1/4 in) long strips

Use a fork to prick the skin on the chicken in several places. Place the chicken, skin side up, in a shallow dish, then pour over the combined sake, lemon juice, ginger and 1 teaspoon salt. Cover and marinate in the refrigerator for 30 minutes.

Combine the shoyu, mirin, sesame oil and spring onion in a small bowl and set aside.

Line a steamer with baking paper. Arrange the chicken, skin side up, in the steamer. Fill a saucepan with 500 ml (17 fl oz/2 cups) water and sit the steamer over the top. Cover and cook over simmering water for 20 minutes, or until cooked.

Cut the chicken into bite-sized pieces, put into a serving bowl and drizzle with the shoyu mixture. Garnish with the capsicum strips and extra spring onion. Serve with rice.

In ancient times, sake was brewed for the gods and shamans alone. Today this popular alcoholic beverage, also called *nihonshu*, is an ideal accompaniment to many Japanese dishes. Its alcohol content ranges from 16–19 per cent, and it is produced in amazing variety by some 2000 breweries. Customarily served warm in the winter, heating helps to improve the taste of lower quality sake. The best, however, are most delicious when served at room temperature or chilled. Sake is often explained as 'rice wine' but because it is brewed it is not a true wine. In certain dishes, however, it is used as a seasoning, just as wine is used in French cooking.

tempura

TEMPURA WAS NOT AN ORIGINAL JAPANESE DISH, BUT WAS INSPIRED BY THE BATTER-FRIED FISH MEALS OF EARLY PORTUGUESE TRADERS. THESE FEATHER-LIGHT, CRISPY PIECES OF SEAFOOD AND VEGETABLES MAKE A DELIGHTFUL DISH. TWO BATCHES OF TEMPURA BATTER ARE NEEDED HERE — MAKE EACH BATCH JUST BEFORE YOU USE IT.

raw king prawns (shrimp)	8, peeled, deveined, tails intact
squid	200 g (7 oz) piece, opened out flat
white fish fillet	200 g (7 oz), cut into 4 even pieces
onion	1/2 small, cut into 4 thin wedges, with a toothpick securing each wedge
jap (kent) pumpkin	4 very thin slices, unpeeled
fresh shiitake mushrooms	4, stems discarded
baby eggplant (aubergine)	1, cut into 5 mm (1/4 in) thick slices on the diagonal
green capsicum (pepper)	1/2 small, cut lengthways into quarters
shiso leaves	4, optional

tempura batter (makes 1 batch)

iced water	310 ml (10 3/4 fl oz/1 1/4 cups)
potato starch	45 g (1 1/2 oz/1/4 cup), sifted
plain (all-purpose) flour	140 g (5 oz/1 heaped cup), sifted
baking powder	1/4 teaspoon
vegetable oil	for deep-frying
sesame oil	60 ml (2 fl oz/1/4 cup)
plain (all-purpose) flour	for coating
tempura dipping sauce	ready-made or see recipe on page 131
daikon	70 g (2 1/2 oz), peeled, finely grated, then squeezed to remove excess liquid
fresh ginger	2 teaspoons finely grated

Make three cuts in the belly of the prawns. Turn the prawns over and, starting from the tail end, press down gently at intervals along the length of the prawn — this helps to break the connective tissue, preventing the prawns from curling up too much. Finely score the squid in a crisscross pattern on both sides, then cut into 4 x 3 cm (1 1/2 x 1 1/4 in) pieces. Arrange the seafood and vegetables on separate platters, cover with plastic wrap and refrigerate until ready to use.

To make one batch of the tempura batter, pour the iced water into a bowl. Add the sifted potato starch, flour, baking powder and 1/4 teaspoon salt all at once and give just a few strokes with a pair of chopsticks to loosely combine. There should be flour all around the edges of the bowl and the batter should be lumpy. (If your kitchen is hot, place the bowl over a bowl of iced water.)

Fill a deep-fat fryer or large saucepan one-third full of vegetable oil, then add the sesame oil. Heat to 180°C (350°F), or until a cube of bread dropped into the oil browns in 15 seconds.

Dip each ingredient into the flour (except the shiso leaves) before dipping it into the batter. Dip the shiso directly into the batter. Starting with the onion and pumpkin, quickly dip into the tempura batter, allowing the excess to drip off, then lower into the oil. Cook for 2–3 minutes, or until cooked through and the batter is lightly golden and crispy. It should also look lacy and a little see-through — if the batter is too thick, add a little more iced water. Drain on paper towels, then keep warm in a low oven while you cook the rest of the vegetables. Skim off any bits of floating batter as you cook.

Make a second batch of batter and cook the seafood in small batches for 1–3 minutes, or until just cooked through and lightly golden and crisp. Keep warm in the oven. Serve with a small bowl of the tempura dipping sauce with grated daikon and ginger mixed in according to taste.

teppanyaki .... serves 4

STEAK AND VEGETABLES PREPARED ON A HOT *TEPPAN*, AN IRON PLATE OR SHEET, ARE A REAL TASTE TREAT, BUT NEVER MORE SO THAN WHEN THEY ARE COOKED RIGHT AT THE TABLE WHERE DINERS CAN NOT ONLY ENJOY THE COLOURS AND AROMAS BUT ALSO SHARE WARM COMPANIONSHIP AND CONVERSATION.

scotch fillet (rib eye)	350 g (12 oz), partially frozen
slender eggplants (aubergines)	4 small
fresh shiitake mushrooms	100 g (3½ oz)
green beans	100 g (3½ oz) small
yellow or green baby (pattypan) squash	6
red or green capsicum (pepper)	1, seeded
spring onions (scallions)	6
bamboo shoots	200 g (7 oz) tinned, drained
oil	60 ml (2 fl oz/¼ cup)
sesame seed sauce	ready-made or see recipe on page 131

Slice the steak into very thin pieces. Place the meat slices in a single layer on a large serving platter and season thoroughly with plenty of salt and freshly ground black pepper. Set aside.

Trim the ends from the eggplants and cut the flesh into long, very thin diagonal slices. Trim any hard stems from the mushrooms. Top and tail the beans. If the beans are longer than 7 cm (2¾ in), cut them in half. Quarter, halve or leave the baby squash whole, depending on the size. Cut the capsicum into thin strips. Remove the outer layer of the spring onions and slice into lengths about 7 cm (2¾ in) long, discarding the tops. Arrange the vegetables in separate bundles on the platter.

When the diners are seated, heat a portable tabletop grill or electric frying pan until very hot, then lightly brush it with the oil. Quickly fry a quarter of the meat, searing on both sides, and then push it over to the edge of the pan. Add about a quarter of the vegetables and quickly stir-fry, adding a little more oil as needed.

Serve a small portion of the meat and vegetables to the diners, along with the sesame seed sauce, for dipping. Repeat the process with the remaining meat and vegetables, cooking in batches as extra helpings are required. Serve with steamed rice.

Season the slices of steak with salt and pepper

Cut the eggplants into very thin slices, cutting on the diagonal

Remove the outer layer of the spring onions before slicing them

yakitori .... makes 8

YAKI MEANS GRILLED (BROILED) AND *TORI* MEANS CHICKEN, BUT ALTHOUGH *YAKITORI* REFERS TO ALL SORTS OF SKEWERED FOODS, CHICKEN REMAINS AMONG THE MOST POPULAR. THESE DELICIOUS MORSELS CAN MAKE A MEAL WITH SIDES, OR PROVIDE A SNACK FOR DRINKS, PARTICULARLY SAKE.

sauce

chicken wings	500 g (1 lb 2 oz), cut into pieces at the joints
mirin	375 ml (13 fl oz/1½ cups)
sake	250 ml (9 fl oz/1 cup)
shoyu (Japanese soy sauce)	375 ml (13 fl oz/1½ cups)
caster (superfine) sugar	55 g (2 oz/¼ cup)
kuzu starch rocks or arrowroot	3 teaspoons
large boneless, skinless chicken thighs	500 g (1 lb 2 oz)
baby leeks or thick spring onions (scallions)	4, white part only, cut into 4 pieces

Soak eight small bamboo skewers in water for 1 hour. To make the sauce, preheat the grill (broiler) to high. Cook the chicken wings, turning occasionally, for 15 minutes, or until dark golden and starting to blacken slightly. Remove and set aside. Pour the mirin and sake into a saucepan over high heat and bring to the boil. Add the shoyu and sugar and stir until the sugar has dissolved. Add the wings and bring the liquid to the boil, then reduce to a simmer for 30 minutes. Remove the pan from the heat and allow to cool for 30 minutes. Strain the sauce (you can serve the chicken wings as a snack). Pour a little of the sauce into a small dish and add the kuzu. Crush the rocks and stir into the sauce until dissolved, then return to the pan. Put the pan over high heat and stir until the mixture boils and becomes thick and glossy. Remove from the heat and allow to cool before using.

Cut each chicken thigh into 12 even pieces. Starting with a piece of chicken, and alternating with the leek, thread three pieces of chicken and two pieces of leek onto each skewer. Pour a little of the sauce into a dish for basting and reserve the rest for serving.

Heat the grill to high and cook the skewers, turning regularly, for 3–4 minutes, then baste with the sauce. Cook on each side for a further 1–2 minutes, basting again, until well glazed and the chicken is cooked through. Serve with a drizzle of the sauce.

Cook the chicken wings until they are dark golden

Add the chicken wings to the liquid in the pan

Baste the chicken and leek skewers with the sauce

crumbed skewers .... serves 4

SKEWERED FOODS ARE CASUAL AND FUN TO EAT, AND THESE PORTIONS OF MEAT, SEAFOOD AND VEGETABLES, CRUMBED AND DEEP-FRIED, OFFER A GREAT TWIST ON CLASSIC YAKITORI. LIFT THE FLAVOUR ANOTHER NOTCH WITH FRUITY TONKATSU SAUCE AND SPICY JAPANESE MUSTARD.

skewers

scallops	8 small, roe removed
raw prawns (shrimp)	4, peeled, deveined, tails intact
pork fillet	225 g (8 oz), cut into 3 x 2 cm (1 1/4 x 3/4 in) pieces about 1 cm (1/2 in) thick
spring onions (scallions)	2, white part only, cut into 3 cm (1 1/4 in) lengths
jap (kent) pumpkin	4 small, unpeeled slices, 5 mm (1/4 in) thick
beef fillet	225 g (8 oz), cut into 3 x 2 cm (1 1/4 x 3/4 in) pieces about 1 cm (1/2 in) thick
firm fish fillets (such as snapper, salmon, tuna or swordfish)	175 g (6 oz), cut into 3 x 2 cm (1 1/4 x 3/4 in) pieces
ground white pepper	pinch
plain (all-purpose) flour	for dusting
egg	1, lightly beaten
panko (Japanese breadcrumbs)	for coating
vegetable oil	for deep-frying
sesame oil	60 ml (2 fl oz/1/4 cup), optional
tonkatsu sauce	ready-made or see recipe on page 124
lemon wedges	to serve
Japanese mustard	to serve
English cabbage leaves	cut into 3 x 2 cm (1 1/4 x 3/4 in) pieces

Soak 24 bamboo skewers in water for 1 hour. Use four skewers for each group of ingredients. Use the following list as a guide to what should go on each skewer: two scallops; one prawn threaded lengthways so the tail is at the top of the skewer; alternating pieces of pork (three pieces) and spring onion (two pieces); one slice of pumpkin; three pieces of beef; three pieces of fish.

Lightly season each skewer with salt and white pepper, then coat with the flour, shaking off any excess. Dip into the beaten egg, allowing any excess to drip off, then press into the crumbs to coat well. Refrigerate until needed.

Fill a deep-fat fryer or large saucepan half-full with the vegetable oil and add the sesame oil, if using. Heat to 170°C (325°F), or until a cube of bread dropped into the oil browns in 20 seconds. Cook a few skewers at a time, lowering them into the oil and cooking until golden and crisp. Cooking time will vary with each ingredient but should take 1–3 minutes. Drain on paper towels.

Serve with tonkatsu sauce, lemon wedges, mustard and a small bowl of the cabbage. For a more substantial meal, serve with rice, miso soup and pickles.

teriyaki chicken .... serves 4

TERIYAKI SAUCE GIVES CHICKEN AN ATTRACTIVE AND DELICIOUS GLAZE THAT PROVES ITS LITERAL MEANING: 'LUSTRE GRILLING (BROILING)'. IT IS SO SIMPLE TO MAKE THAT IT SEEMS UNIMAGINABLE THAT THE INSTANT BOTTLED SAUCES WOULD HAVE EVER FOUND A MARKET.

shoyu (Japanese soy sauce)	60 ml (2 fl oz/1/4 cup)
mirin	2 tablespoons
sake	2 tablespoons
caster (superfine) sugar	1 1/2 tablespoons
vegetable oil	2 teaspoons
boneless chicken thighs	4 x 200 g (7 oz) with skin, or cutlets with the bone removed

Combine the shoyu, mirin, sake and sugar in a small bowl and stir until the sugar has dissolved. Set aside.

Heat the oil in a large, heavy-based frying pan over medium–high heat. Add the chicken, skin side down, and cook for 4–5 minutes, or until the skin is golden. Turn the chicken over and cook for a further 3–4 minutes, or until golden and almost cooked through. Remove from the pan.

Discard any excess fat from the pan, then pour in the shoyu mixture, increase the heat to high and bring to the boil. Cook for 1 minute, or until the liquid has slightly reduced and is glossy. Return the chicken and any juices to the pan and turn to coat well. Remove from the pan and slice on a slight angle into 1.5 cm (5/8 in) wide strips. Holding the chicken thighs in their original shape, transfer to a plate or bowl. Serve with rice and vegetables or a salad.

Soy sauce, *shoyu*, is so valued in Japanese cuisine that it is usually referred to with the honorific 'o' prefix. Indeed, soy sauce is used as commonly in Japan as salt is used in the West. *O-shoyu* is made from a fermentation of soya beans, wheat, water and salt. Of the several main varieties, *koikuchi shoyu*, the regular dark sauce, is most widely used, whereas *usukuchi shoyu*, a light-coloured sauce, is useful for dishes in which a darker sauce might give an unappealing or 'dirty' appearance. *Tamari-joyu*, an intense, dark, slightly thicker sauce, usually made without wheat, is the dipping sauce of choice for sashimi. The best quality soy sauces can take up to 2 years to make.

yakisoba .... serves 4

YAKISOBA IS EASY TO MAKE AT HOME IN A WOK — STIR-FRY THE MEAT AND VEGETABLES WITH THE NOODLES AND THEN MELD THEM ALL TOGETHER WITH A SAVOURY SAUCE. THIS NOODLE DISH IS ALSO A POPULAR STREET STALL FOOD IN JAPAN.

dried shiitake mushrooms	4
beef fillet steak or pork fillet	300 g (10½ oz), thinly sliced across the grain
garlic	3 cloves, finely chopped
fresh ginger	3 teaspoons finely chopped
yakisoba noodles	500 g (1 lb 2 oz)
bacon	6 slices, cut into 3 cm (1¼ in) squares
vegetable oil	2 tablespoons
sesame oil	1 teaspoon
spring onions (scallions)	6, cut into 3 cm (1¼ in) lengths
carrot	1, thinly sliced on the diagonal
green capsicum (pepper)	1 small, cut into thin strips
Chinese cabbage	250 g (9 oz), thinly sliced
bamboo shoots	100 g (3½ oz), thinly sliced
pickled ginger	1 tablespoon thinly sliced
nori flakes or strips	to serve, optional
fine katsuobushi (bonito flakes)	to serve, optional

sauce

shoyu (Japanese soy sauce)	60 ml (2 fl oz/¼ cup)
worcestershire sauce	2 tablespoons
Japanese rice vinegar	1½ tablespoons
sake	1 tablespoon
mirin	1 tablespoon
tomato sauce (ketchup)	1 tablespoon
oyster sauce	1 tablespoon
black or dark brown sugar	2 teaspoons

Soak the shiitake in hot water for 30 minutes. Drain, reserving 2 tablespoons of the soaking liquid. Discard the stems and thinly slice the caps. Meanwhile, put the beef in a large bowl with half the garlic and half the fresh ginger and mix well. Put the yakisoba noodles in a colander and pour boiling water over them. Drain the noodles and separate.

To make the sauce, combine all the ingredients in a bowl with the reserved mushroom liquid and the remaining garlic and ginger.

Heat a wok over medium–high heat, add the bacon and stir-fry for 3 minutes, or until starting to soften and brown. Set aside in a large bowl. Combine the vegetable and sesame oils in a bowl. Increase the heat to high and add a little of the oil mixture, then stir-fry the beef for 1 minute, or until it starts to change colour all over. Add to the bacon. Add a little more oil to the wok, then stir-fry the shiitake, spring onion, carrot, capsicum, cabbage and bamboo shoots for 1–2 minutes, or until the vegetables are just cooked but still crisp. Add to the bowl with the meat. Add the remaining oil to the wok and stir-fry the noodles for 1 minute. Return the meat and vegetables to the wok, add the sauce and pickled ginger and stir-fry for 2–3 minutes, or until heated through. Serve garnished with nori and katsuobushi, if using.

Pour boiling water over the noodles, then drain

Stir-fry the vegetables until just cooked but still crisp

japanese curry

CURRY, OF INDIAN ORIGIN, WAS INTRODUCED VIA THE ENGLISH, MEANING THAT IT WAS A LITTLE TRANSFORMED, NOT ONCE BUT TWICE. JAPANESE CURRY, SUITED WELL TO JAPANESE TASTES, IS A POPULAR RESTAURANT LUNCH-ON-THE-RUN AS WELL AS A FAVOURITE FAMILY DISH.

butter	25 g (1 oz)
sesame oil	1 teaspoon
vegetable oil	2 tablespoons
onion	1 large, cut in half, then sliced into 1 cm (1/2 in) wedges
pork or lamb shoulder or chuck steak	750 g (1 lb 10 oz), cut into 3 cm (1 1/4 in) cubes
ground white pepper	pinch
garlic	2 cloves, crushed
Japanese curry powder	1 1/2 tablespoons
dashi II	375 ml (13 fl oz/1 1/2 cups) (see recipe on page 24)
mirin	2 tablespoons
shoyu (Japanese soy sauce)	1 tablespoon
white miso paste	3 tablespoons
all-purpose potatoes	2 large, cut into 2 cm (3/4 in) cubes
carrots	2, cut in half lengthways, then cut into 3 cm (1 1/4 in) pieces
green beans	100 g (3 1/2 oz), trimmed and cut into 4 cm (1 1/2 in) lengths
pickles	to serve

Heat the butter, sesame oil and half the vegetable oil in a large saucepan over medium heat. Add the onion and cook, stirring regularly, for 10–15 minutes, or until golden. Remove from the pan and set aside.

Pour the remaining vegetable oil into the pan. Season the meat with salt and white pepper, then cook in batches for 5–7 minutes, or until browned all over. Remove from the pan and set aside.

Add the garlic and curry powder to the pan and stir for 1 minute, or until fragrant. Return the onion and meat to the pan and stir to coat with the curry. Pour in the dashi, mirin, shoyu and 500 ml (17 fl oz/2 cups) water, then stir in the miso. Bring to the boil, then reduce to a simmer and cook for 1 hour. Add the potato and carrot and cook for a further 50 minutes. Add the beans and cook for 10 minutes, or until all the vegetables are very tender. Season to taste and serve with rice or noodles, accompanied by pickles of your choice.

Cut the onion in half, then slice each half into wedges

Cook the meat for 1 hour, then add the potato and carrot

Add the beans to the curry and cook for 10 minutes

desserts

At the conclusion of a meal in Japan, thoughts do not habitually turn to dessert. Both sweet and savoury elements are usually present within a traditional meal, but if any sweet takes a closing bow at all, it would most often be seasonal fresh fruit. It could be a persimmon or pear, always peeled, perfectly sliced and presented on a dish, rather than eaten out of hand. Or on a cold winter evening, perhaps a *mikan* (tangerine) eaten while watching TV and cozily warming one's legs beneath the blanket of the *kotatsu* table.

Dezaato is a foreign concept, and a true Japanese sweet would never be associated with that word. 'Dessert' only describes what is otherwise called *yogashi*, a Western-style confection typically utilizing wheat flour, eggs and dairy products such as butter, cream or milk. The Japanese usually enjoy their sweets as *o-yatsu*, an afternoon tea-time snack. Although in recent years Western pastries, cakes and cookies have become immensely popular, but they are often made in a lighter version to appeal to Japanese tastes.

Some of the ingredients used in *wagashi*, Japanese sweets, are rice, millet and soya flours, sweet potatoes, chestnuts, beans, seeds and nuts. Many of the sweets are as simple as dumplings with a flavourful filling or coating, while others are so beautifully designed that they are like edible works of art. The sweetness of these traditional morsels provides a foil for the slight bitterness of the popular everyday green tea beverage which they often accompany.

Gelatine desserts, called *zeli*, are popular, particularly in summer because of their light taste and cool appearance. Usually fruit flavoured, they are moulded in individual cups. Often suspended within are a few perfect pieces of the fruit itself. A particularly luxurious one has a whole steamed apple moulded into the apple-flavoured gelatine. Packed in boxes, these make wonderful summer gifts.

Cuisine is, however, an ever-changing thing, and in our well-travelled world, influences and inspirations abound. The culinary fusion trend of recent years has chefs and cooks everywhere playing with the infinite flavours and techniques of East and West. Occasionally these mix-and-match experiments produce surprising and delightful results, like ices and ice creams with quintessential Japanese flavours, or new versions of favourite Euro-style pastries with Eastern fillings. These creative desserts appeal to our broadening tastes and give a sweet ending to special Japanese meals.

plum wine granita .... serves 6

FOR A REFRESHING CLOSE TO A SOPHISTICATED DINNER ON A HOT SUMMER EVENING, THIS GRANITA IS AN IDEAL CHOICE. FRUITY, WITH A TART SWEETNESS AND A HINT OF GINGER, AS WELL AS LIGHTLY ALCOHOLIC, THIS BRIGHT DESSERT MAKES A BEAUTIFUL PRESENTATION.

caster (superfine) sugar	115 g (4 oz/^{1}/2 cup)
lemon zest	a few strips
young fresh ginger	2 cm (^{3}/4 in) piece, thinly sliced
ripe plums	500 g (1 lb 2 oz), seeded
Japanese plum wine	500 ml (17 fl oz/2 cups)

Combine the sugar with the lemon zest, ginger and 375 ml (13 fl oz/1^1/2 cups) water. Stir over high heat until the sugar has dissolved, then bring to the boil. Reduce the heat to low and simmer for 10 minutes. Cool completely, then strain.

Purée the plum flesh in a food processor, then strain through a fine sieve to extract the juice — you will need about 250 ml (9 fl oz/1 cup). Add to the cooled syrup with the plum wine, then pour into a shallow 30 x 20 cm (12 x 8 in) metal container. Place in the freezer until the mixture begins to freeze around the edges.

Remove from the freezer and scrape the frozen sections back into the mixture with a fork. Repeat every 30 minutes, until the mixture has even-sized ice crystals. Just before serving, beat the mixture with a fork, then spoon into six bowls or glasses.

Umeshu is commonly called 'plum wine' in English, but technically it is neither wine nor precisely of plums. The *ume* is really a kind of apricot. Due to its high acidity, it is not eaten raw, but in early summer the green fruits are ready to be made into a delightful liqueur. Although produced commercially, *umeshu* is also popularly made at home. Layered with rock sugar, and immersed in white liquor, the fruit is left to macerate and ferment in a cool, dark place. In 3 months it is ready to drink and, imbibed as an aperitif, is considered very beneficial to the health. This traditional liqueur is sometimes used to create contemporary cocktails and some desserts.

nashi and ginger strudel . . . . serves 6–8

THE CRISPY APPLE-SHAPED JAPANESE PEAR MAKES AN EXCELLENT STRUDEL FILLING, ITS FLAVOUR ACCENTED BY AROMATIC GINGER. THE CHOPPED WALNUTS AND SESAME SEEDS SCATTERED BETWEEN BUTTERY LAYERS OF PASTRY, AND THE TOUCH OF KINAKO ON TOP, ADD EVEN MORE APPEAL.

nashi pears	4 small, peeled, cored and sliced
lemon juice	1 tablespoon
fresh ginger	2 teaspoons finely grated
panko (Japanese breadcrumbs)	30 g (1 oz/1/2 cup)
caster (superfine) sugar	230 g (8 oz/1 cup)
sesame seeds	40 g (1 1/2 oz/1/4 cup), lightly toasted, plus extra to garnish
walnuts	50 g (1 3/4 oz/1/2 cup), very finely chopped
ground cinnamon	1 1/2 teaspoons
ground ginger	1 teaspoon
filo pastry	8 sheets
unsalted butter	150 g (5 1/2 oz), melted
icing (confectioners') sugar	2 tablespoons
kinako (roasted soya bean flour)	2 tablespoons

Preheat the oven to 180°C (350°F/Gas 4). Lightly grease a baking tray. Put the nashi slices in a bowl with the lemon juice, fresh ginger, panko and half the sugar and stir well. Combine the sesame seeds, walnuts, cinnamon, ground ginger and remaining sugar in a separate bowl.

Lay one sheet of filo on a work surface with the long edge towards you, brush lightly with a little melted butter, then lay another sheet on top so it overlaps the edge furthest away from you by about 5 cm (2 in). Brush with a little more butter. Sprinkle about one-quarter of the sesame mixture over the top of the two pastry sheets, then keep layering in the same position with the rest of the filo and sesame mix, brushing each sheet of pastry with melted butter.

Leave a 4 cm (1 1/2 in) border along the edge of the pastry closest to you and on both sides, and place the nashi mixture in a neat log along the edge closest to you. Carefully roll up, folding in the sides about halfway along, then continue rolling to the end.

Carefully transfer the strudel to the prepared tray, seam side down, and brush all over with melted butter. Bake for 50 minutes, or until golden. Allow to cool slightly before sprinkling with sifted combined icing sugar and kinako. Slice on the diagonal and serve with lightly whipped cream, if desired.

Combine the nashi, lemon juice, fresh ginger, panko and sugar

Roll up the filo pastry to enclose the nashi mixture

Tuck in the sides of the pastry, then continue rolling to the end

black sesame ice cream .... serves 4

SESAME IS ONE OF JAPAN'S BEST-LOVED TASTES, AND IT FINDS ITS WAY INTO A GREAT VARIETY OF FOODS, BOTH SAVOURY AND SWEET. TOASTED AND CRUSHED SEEDS ATTRACTIVELY FLECK THIS ICE CREAM, AND THEIR MILD NUTTINESS COMPLEMENTS ITS DELICIOUS SWEETNESS.

black sesame seeds	2 tablespoons
milk	750 ml (26 fl oz/3 cups)
cream (whipping)	250 ml (9 fl oz/1 cup)
sugar	165 g (5¾ oz/¾ cup)
egg yolks	2

Heat a non-stick frying pan over high heat and dry-fry the black sesame seeds for 2–3 minutes, or until the seeds begin to pop, shaking the pan so the seeds cook evenly. Remove from the pan and allow to cool. When cool, grind the seeds in a mortar and pestle or a spice mill to form a rough powder.

Heat the milk, cream, half of the sugar and the ground sesame seeds in a saucepan, stirring constantly, until the mixture reaches boiling point. Remove from the heat.

Beat the egg yolks with the remaining sugar for 3–4 minutes, or until pale and thick and add 125 ml (4 fl oz/½ cup) of the warm milk mixture to the egg mixture and beat for 1 minute. Gradually pour in the remaining milk mixture, beating constantly. Pour the mixture into a clean saucepan and cook over low heat for 8–10 minutes, stirring constantly until the mixture has thickened and coats the back of the spoon. Pour into a large bowl, cover and refrigerate until cool.

Pour the cooled mixture into an ice-cream machine and churn according to the manufacturer's instructions until the mixture is frozen. If making by hand, freeze until frozen around the edges but not in the centre, then beat with an electric mixer to break down any ice crystals. Return to the freezer and repeat this process at least twice more.

Grind the toasted sesame seeds to form a rough powder

Heat the milk, cream, half the sugar and ground sesame seeds

Beat the egg yolks with the sugar until pale and thick

three ways with green tea

O-CHA, GREEN TEA, ARRIVED IN JAPAN WITH BUDDHISM SOME 1500 YEARS AGO, BUT WAS INITIALLY VALUED ONLY FOR ITS MEDICINAL PROPERTIES AND AS AN AID TO MEDITATION. TODAY, COUNTLESS MILLIONS OF CUPS OF IT ARE CONSUMED EACH DAY. IT IS ALSO A POPULAR FLAVOURING INGREDIENT FOR FOODS SUCH AS RICE CRACKERS, SOBA NOODLE DOUGH, ICE CREAM AND OTHER SWEETS. MOST FAMOUSLY, GREEN TEA IS PREPARED IN A FORMAL CEREMONY CALLED SADO, IN WHICH POWDERED TEA IS VIGOROUSLY WHISKED INTO A FROTHY BEVERAGE.

white chocolate and green tea cakes

Preheat the oven to 180°C (350°F/Gas 4). Lightly grease a 12-hole patty cake tin. Put 50 g (1¾ oz) chopped white chocolate and 50 g (1¾ oz) chopped unsalted butter in a large heatproof bowl over simmering water. Stir until smooth, then remove from the heat. Stir 1 teaspoon matcha (green tea powder) in 50 ml (1¾ fl oz) hot water until dissolved and add to the chocolate mixture with 115 g (4 oz/½ cup) caster (superfine) sugar. Beat for 1 minute, or until combined. Add 1 lightly beaten egg to the mixture and beat for 1 minute. Stir in 125 g (4½ oz/1 cup) sifted plain (all-purpose) flour and ½ teaspoon baking powder. Spoon the mixture into the prepared cake tin and bake for 15 minutes. Allow to cool before removing the cakes from the tin. Combine ½ teaspoon matcha and 1 tablespoon icing (confectioners') sugar and sieve over the cakes before serving. Makes 12.

green tea ice cream

Pour 250 ml (9 fl oz/1 cup) milk and 625 ml (21½ fl oz/2½ cups) cream (whipping) into a saucepan with 1 vanilla bean split in half lengthways. Bring just to the boil over medium–high heat. Remove from the heat and allow the vanilla to infuse into the milk mixture for 15 minutes. Put 9 egg yolks and 145 g (5 oz/⅔ cup) caster (superfine) sugar in a bowl and beat until creamy. Slowly pour in the milk mixture, whisking as you pour, until smooth. Pour into a clean saucepan and put the pan over medium heat. Stir for 10 minutes, or until it is just thick enough to coat the back of a spoon. Put 3 teaspoons matcha (green tea powder) in a small bowl, stir in enough of the hot custard to form a paste, then add to the rest of the custard, whisking until smooth and an even green colour. Strain through a fine sieve and cool slightly. Cover and refrigerate until completely chilled, then churn in an ice-cream machine according to the manufacturer's instructions. Place in the freezer until ready to use. If making by hand, freeze until frozen around the edges but not in the centre, then whisk with an electric whisk to break down any ice crystals. Return to the freezer and repeat this process at least twice more. The more times it is beaten while freezing the finer and silkier the finished texture will be. The finished ice cream should be light, not icy. Makes 1 litre (35 fl oz/4 cups).

iced green tea with soy milk

Combine 250 ml (9 fl oz/1 cup) water, 75 g (2½ oz/⅓ cup) sugar and 1 teaspoon matcha (green tea powder) in a small saucepan and bring to the boil, stirring until the sugar has dissolved. Remove from the heat and pour into a bowl. Refrigerate until needed. Place several cubes of ice in four tall glasses and pour over the chilled green tea mixture. Top with chilled soya milk and serve. Serves 4.

white chocolate and green tea cakes

banana tempura .... serves 4

BATTER-FRIED BANANAS ARE A FURTHER TAKE ON THE TEMPURA TECHNIQUE, WHICH LENDS ITSELF NICELY TO A BROAD VARIETY OF INGREDIENTS. SERVED WARM WITH HONEY AND ICE CREAM, OR JUST WITH A CUP OF GREEN TEA, THEY MAKE A DELIGHTFUL DESSERT.

oil	for deep-frying
egg	1
iced water	185 ml (6 fl oz/^{3}/$_4$ cup)
tempura flour	90 g (3^1/$_4$ oz/^{2}/$_3$ cup)
bananas	4 small
caster (superfine) sugar	to serve
warmed honey	to serve

Fill a deep-fat fryer or large saucepan one-third full of oil. Heat to 170°C (325°F), or until a cube of bread dropped into the oil browns in 20 seconds.

Mix together the egg and iced water in a bowl, then stir in the tempura flour. Do not whisk the batter — it should be lumpy.

Split the bananas in half lengthways, then in half crossways. Dip the banana quarters into the batter and deep-fry a few at a time for about 2 minutes, or until crisp and golden. Drain on paper towels and sprinkle with sugar. Drizzle with warmed honey and serve with a scoop of sesame seed ice cream or green tea ice cream (see recipes on page 178 or 181).

Gently stir the tempura flour into the egg and iced water

Dip the pieces of banana into the tempura batter

Deep-fry the bananas, a few at a time, until crisp and golden

japanese apple
and pear crumble .... serves 4

A BELOVED BAKED DESSERT, FRUIT CRUMBLE, IS GIVEN A JAPANESE TWIST WITH THE USE OF BOTH NASHI PEARS AND FUJI APPLES. MORE FLAVOUR AND AROMA ARE ADDED TO THE CRISPY BROWN SUGAR TOPPING WITH THE ADDITION OF SESAME SEEDS AND KINAKO.

fuji apples	3
nashi pears	3
lemon juice	2 teaspoons
sugar	2 tablespoons
cornflour (cornstarch)	1 tablespoon
white sesame seeds	1 tablespoon, toasted
kinako (roasted soya bean flour)	2 tablespoons
plain (all-purpose) flour	2 tablespoons
ground cinnamon	1 teaspoon
unsalted butter	50 g (1³/4 oz), cut into small cubes and chilled
soft brown sugar	115 g (4 oz/¹/2 cup)

Preheat the oven to 200°C (400°F/Gas 6). Lightly grease four 250 ml (9 fl oz/1 cup) ramekins.

Peel the apples and nashi and slice the flesh. Put the fruit in a bowl with the lemon juice, sugar and cornflour. Toss to combine, then transfer to a saucepan with 60 ml (2 fl oz/¹/4 cup) water. Cover and cook over medium heat for 5 minutes, stirring often. Leave to cool for 5 minutes with the lid on, then spoon the mixture into the ramekins.

Roughly grind the sesame seeds in a spice mill or using a mortar and pestle. Put the sesame seeds in a bowl with the kinako, flour, cinnamon, butter and brown sugar. Using your fingertips, rub the mixture until it resembles coarse breadcrumbs.

Sprinkle over the fruit and bake for 20–25 minutes, or until dark around the edge. Remove from the oven and serve.

Rub the cubes of butter into the sesame seed and flour mixture

Continue to rub the mixture until it resembles coarse breadcrumbs

pancakes with sweet adzuki bean paste

.... makes 6

SWEET RED BEAN PASTE IS A POPULAR FILLING FOR A GREAT VARIETY OF JAPANESE CONFECTIONS. THESE DELICIOUS SANDWICH-STYLE TREATS ARE PARTICULARLY EASY AND QUICK TO MAKE, AND THE PANCAKES MAKE A PERFECT FOIL FOR THE SWEETNESS OF THE FILLING.

plain (all-purpose) flour	125 g (4$\frac{1}{2}$ oz/1 cup)
baking powder	1 teaspoon
caster (superfine) sugar	2 tablespoons
eggs	2
milk	125 ml (4 fl oz/$\frac{1}{2}$ cup)
unsalted butter	25 g (1 oz)
oil	1 tablespoon
anko (sweet adzuki bean paste)	150 g (5$\frac{1}{2}$ oz/$\frac{1}{2}$ cup)

Sift the flour and baking powder into a bowl and stir in the sugar. Combine the eggs and milk and whisk well. Make a well in the flour, pour in the egg mixture and stir until well combined.

Heat a little of the butter and oil in a frying pan over medium–high heat until the butter has melted. Cooking in batches, drop about 2 tablespoons of the batter per pancake (spread to a diameter of 9 cm/3$\frac{1}{2}$ in) into the pan and cook for 2 minutes, or until there are lots of bubbles on the surface. Turn over and cook a further 30 seconds. Don't worry if the first couple don't work. Remove from the pan, cover and set aside while you cook the remaining pancakes. You should end up with 12 good pancakes.

Sandwich two pancakes together with about 1 tablespoon of the anko and repeat with the remaining pancakes and filling. Serve warm or at room temperature with green tea as an afternoon or after-dinner treat.

Sweet adzuki paste, called *an* or *anko*, is a favoured ingredient in Japanese confections. It is a popular filling for such treats as *mochi* rice cakes, and also for the street stall snacks called *tai yaki*, a waffle-like treat made in the shape of the *tai* fish or sea bream. This paste often surprises many foreign visitors to Japan. When, after a time, they begin to feel the need for some familiar comfort food, they may eagerly bite into what appears to be a chocolate-filled pastry, only to discover that the 'fudge' is sweet bean paste. *Anko* can be purchased ready-made or can be prepared at home, in either smooth or chunky versions.

chocolate pudding
with adzuki heart .... makes 6

A TRULY PERFECT CONCOCTION COMBINING THE FLAVOURS OF BOTH EAST AND WEST, THIS PLEASING CHOCOLATE
BAKED PUDDING FEATURES A HEART OF CHOCOLATE-INFUSED SWEET ADZUKI BEAN PASTE. A SPRINKLE OF COCOA
POWDER GIVES THIS DESSERT A CONTRASTING FINISH.

anko (sweet adzuki bean paste)	1 tablespoon
dark cooking chocolate	150 g (5½ oz), chopped
unsalted butter	125 g (4½ oz), chopped
plain (all-purpose) flour	90 g (3¼ oz/¾ cup)
caster (superfine) sugar	80 g (2¾ oz/⅓ cup)
baking powder	½ teaspoon
eggs	4, lightly beaten
unsweetened cocoa powder	1 teaspoon

Put the anko and 25 g (1 oz) of the chocolate in a small heatproof bowl over simmering water and stir until melted and combined. Cover and refrigerate for 3 hours.

Put the remaining chocolate and butter in a heatproof bowl and place over a saucepan of simmering water for 10–15 minutes, stirring often, until completely melted and combined. Remove from the heat. Combine the flour, sugar and baking powder in a large bowl and beat in the eggs until the mixture is smooth. Beat in the chocolate mixture until smooth. Cover and refrigerate.

Preheat the oven to 220°C (425°F/Gas 7). Grease six 125 ml (4 fl oz/½ cup) ramekins. Spoon enough of the pudding mixture into the ramekin to come two-thirds of the way up the side. Spoon 1 teaspoon of the anko mixture into the middle of each pudding, then spoon over the remaining pudding mixture. Bake for 13–15 minutes, or until the mixture has risen to the top of the ramekins. Remove from the oven and cool for a few minutes. Invert onto a plate, sieve cocoa powder over the top and serve.

Melt the chocolate and butter over simmering water

Spoon a little anko mixture into the middle of the pudding

Invert the cooked puddings onto a serving plate

index

This edition first published in Canada in 2006 by Whitecap Books, 351 Lynn Ave., North Vancouver, British Columbia, Canada, V7J 2C4.

www.whitecap.ca

First published in 2006 by Murdoch Books Pty Limited.

Chief Executive: Juliet Rogers
Publisher: Kay Scarlett

Design concept: Vivien Valk
Design and art direction: Susanne Geppert
Project manager: Paul McNally
Editor: Kim Rowney
Text: Charlotte Anderson
Recipes: Jane Lawson, Ross Dobson and the Murdoch Books Test Kitchen
Photographer: Ian Hofstetter
Stylist: Opel Khan
Food preparation: Ross Dobson
Production: Maiya Levitch

ISBN 1-55285-735-2
ISBN 978-1-55285-735-9

Printed by 1010 Printing International Limited in 2006. PRINTED IN CHINA.

IMPORTANT: Those who might be at risk from the effects of salmonella poisoning (the elderly, pregnant women, young children and those suffering from immune deficiency diseases) should consult their doctor with any concerns about eating raw eggs.

CONVERSION GUIDE: You may find cooking times vary depending on the oven you are using. For fan-forced ovens, as a general rule, set the oven temperature to 20°C (35°F) lower than indicated in the recipe. We have used 20 ml (4 teaspoon) tablespoon measures. If you are using a 15 ml (3 teaspoon) tablespoon, for most recipes the difference will not be noticeable. However, for recipes using baking powder, gelatine, bicarbonate of soda (baking soda), small amounts of flour and cornflour (cornstarch), add an extra teaspoon for each tablespoon specified.